Father Joe

Life Stories of a Hustler Priest

Father Joe Carroll's Memoir

as shared with and written by

Kathryn Cloward

KANDON
UNLIMITED

Father Joe

Life Stories of a Hustler Priest

Father Joe: Life Stories of a Hustler Priest
© 2021 Kathryn Cloward | ℗ 2021 Kandon Unlimited, Inc.
This book is published and distributed by Kandon Unlimited, Inc.
All rights reserved.
Printed in the United States of America.

Library of Congress Number: 2021930842

ISBN 13: 978-1970163629
ISBN 10: 1970163623

Edited by Adrienne Moch
Designed by David Stone
Cover Photos by Carina Fleckner

KANDON
UNLIMITED, INC.
Heart-Centered Mindful Media

This book is dedicated in loving memory to Kitty Carroll.

"Father Joe"

"Father Joe"

A while ago, a group of high school students came to visit and interview me. Before we got started, they wondered how to address me. They had heard about the honor bestowed on me, receiving a Doctorate of Humane Letters from the California State University system at its San Diego State University campus. The students wondered if they should be addressing me as Doctor Carroll instead of Father Joe.

It is amazing to think about how many names and titles we all carry during our lives. For me, the first was within my family as Joseph to Joey to Joe to Uncle Joe. Then in scouting, I was Senior Patrol Leader to Assistant Scoutmaster to Scoutmaster. After ordination, I became Scout Chaplain and later National Scout Chaplain. Many church titles followed: Father, Knight of Columbus, Knight of the Holy Sepulchre, and then Monsignor. At the village, I have had titles of President then President Emeritus. In education, I was known as a student then Bachelor then Master then Doctor. My Jewish friends have always called me a Shabbos goy.

At the time of writing this, I have been a Catholic Carroll for seventy-nine years, a Boy Scout for sixty-seven years, a priest for forty-seven years, and at Father Joe's Villages for thirty-eight years.

Those of you who know me or have met me have probably called me by one or more of these names and titles. For those of you meeting me for the first time by way of this book, you might now be wondering what to call me. To make things easy and simple, I like to be called by the title I use most and that will be on my gravestone, the one I worked hardest to live up to, and that is "Father Joe."

The greatest honor of my life has been being a priest and it's been my desire to follow in the footsteps of Jesus to the best of my ability. In addition to Father Joe, there will be five words on my gravestone: "He was a good priest." It won't say great or exceptional; "good" is the word and good is good enough for me. Perhaps by reading this, you will discover that good is good enough for you in your life, too.

Thank you for taking the time to read my story. I am choosing to share now, as I am almost eighty years old, because I know one of the ways we help each other is through storytelling. By sharing our stories, we are able to understand each other more. When we understand each other more, we are more compassionate with our choices and more open to experiencing the fullness of life through our oneness—who we are together. The Bible is full of stories of people sharing about their experiences of life and God. This book shares stories from my life experiences and how God guided me to be a servant of the people— including being kicked out of the seminary, being fired from jobs, and accepting the moniker of being a "hustler" wheeler and dealer to get the job done.

I have lived a joyful and fulfilling life. Within the pages of this book, I pass along some seeds of goodness to you. Perhaps you will pass seeds of goodness along to others. And so it goes as we help each other grow through life. God bless you today and always. May you experience the joy and fullness of life every day.

Part 1

1.

A Boy From New York

I was born and raised in the Bronx, New York of Irish parents, Jim and Kitty Carroll. There were eight kids, and we all lived with my parents in a two-bedroom apartment, which we thought was big. That was back in 1941. I was born on April 12, 1941. As I share this, it is 2020. I have lived a good life.

It was great to live in the Bronx. I didn't know we were poor until I went to college in California—where people lived more spread out. We were ten people living in a two-bedroom apartment. It was all I knew growing up. We didn't realize it was crowded living as we had four boys in one bedroom, four girls in the other, and my parents sleeping in the living room. We had fun together and our family was extremely loving.

I was close with my brothers and sisters growing up and we are all still close today. In order of our ages, I am in the middle of my siblings, with oldest to youngest being Jack,

Jim, Kathleen, me, Tom, Patsy, Peggy, and Eileen. I credit my parents for raising us to value family. We didn't have much, but we didn't know it. We had each other. Even when we don't agree on things, which happens, we respect and love one another. It's always been that way.

My parents were Irish immigrants in the United States of America. They had two other children who passed away as babies before the eight of us came along, but we never knew of our other sister and brother until we were adults. Our parents never spoke of them. I found out about our sister when I was in my twenties and visiting Ireland for the first time. One day, my aunt asked me, "Do you want to go visit your sister's grave?" Puzzled, I said, "Go visit what? Who?" Our oldest sibling, a sister, died as a baby and was buried in Ireland. Then we also had a brother who died as a baby and we only found this out when one of my sisters was researching our ancestry and discovered a few years ago that we had a brother buried in Brooklyn, New York.

This was all news to us. But that was the Irish way back then, I guess. You just don't talk about some things. If you didn't have much of a life, and they were both babies when they passed, there wasn't anything to talk about or remember. Our parents never spoke of them around us, and perhaps never around each other. We don't know. So, there were really ten siblings in total, but the eight of us grew up together with our parents.

My dad worked as a laborer. He usually had two or three

jobs and worked hard every day earning money to support our family. He was a drinker and if he was left to his own devices, he'd spend everything on booze. That was the selfish part of him, his drinking. Sometimes, he'd come home with bruises and blood on him from getting in a fight at the pub or wherever. But no matter what, he worked every day for his family. It didn't matter if it was snowing outside with ten inches on the ground, he'd get up and walk to work. He had a good work ethic. He instilled that in all of us.

My mom also had an exceptional work ethic. She not only managed the household, raising eight kids, she worked two and three jobs at a time. She cleaned doctors' offices. She'd go in at four or five in the morning to do her cleaning work for a few hours, and then come home to get us all up and fed for school. Once we were on our way, she'd leave to go clean another doctor's office.

Our mom was angelic. How she ever raised eight kids with what we had was amazing. She knew dad's drinking habits and I remember when we were growing up, Mom would send one of us kids down to Dad's job to pick up his paycheck. She knew if nobody picked it up, he'd cash it for booze and none of the money would make it home to pay for food and rent.

As far as I was concerned, I had no idea we were poor. I don't think any of us did at the time. We didn't know anything different. It wasn't until I went to college and had to write a paper on the subject of poverty in New York that I realized what I was writing about included my family. We thought it was normal to live with four kids per room. We never heard of master bedrooms and everyone having their own room, or having a home with a garage. That wasn't what we experienced. But when I was researching about poverty for my college paper, I realized, wow, four kids per bedroom, yes, that's poverty. One of my brothers doesn't like it when I talk about us being poor, but it's the truth. That doesn't mean we didn't have a good life. We did. We had a good life growing up. I had a happy childhood.

2.

Butcher Boy

I learned early in life that if you want money, money is available. All you have to do is work for it. So that is what I did. We didn't have child labor laws then. I got my first job when I was eight years old and I have been working ever since.

I started working for a butcher when I was eight years old. I worked at the butcher shop until I was eighteen, so I was a butcher boy. I helped clean up. I learned how to cut down a complete side of beef and how to make Italian sausage. At the same time, I learned how to cheat, because we would take a chicken and weigh it for a customer, then before packaging it for them to take home, we'd clean up its insides and throw the extra away. Well, part of the "extra" was four-ounce weights we had previously put inside the chicken. Customers would pick out the chicken they wanted, we'd weigh it, and they'd pay based on that weight. After they left, we'd take those weights out of the trash, wash them, and put them into another chicken so it would weigh more for the next customer to pay more. I think about some of the crazy things I did when I was younger, and that nobody saw anything wrong with it.

Every Saturday, my brothers and sisters would line up outside the butcher shop and I'd give them money for movies, because we never had money in the family. We barely got by. At times we couldn't pay rent. I liked working. My instincts were to work and help my family, and that's what I did.

I like doing things. I like keeping busy. This has always been true for me, from the time I was a boy all throughout my life. I can't not be involved. It's not my nature. Working and being busy are part of who I am.

When I worked at the butcher shop, I also took bags of food to people's homes in my neighborhood, especially the old folks who couldn't get out. I liked making sure everyone had what they needed and instinctively just helped. The butcher shop was my first job, and I ultimately was promoted to operate the machinery that chopped meat and ground beef, which was a big deal at the time being just a boy—a butcher boy.

3.

Everyone is Our Neighbor

When I was growing up in the Bronx, nobody was a stranger. It was as a kid that I came to understand the value of being a helpful neighbor and knowing that everyone is our neighbor. Neighbors care for each other and help each other. When Jesus asked, "Who is my neighbor?," his answer to that question was essentially that everyone is my neighbor—and that includes people in need. Living his example means even if I don't know you, you are my neighbor. To treat our neighbors as we want to be treated means everyone, not just people who are like us. Everyone is our neighbor.

That is how I grew up. Our building had ten apartments in it and we knew everyone. We were all Irish and our building neighbors were like one big family. We cared for each other. I don't remember any of us ever locking our door. Everyone was welcome anytime. If my mother wasn't home and I needed something, I went to Maisie's apartment. And if she wasn't home, I went to Rose's. If she was gone, I'd go upstairs to Kathleen's. And it wasn't as if I needed to knock on the door. I just opened the door and walked in like it was my home. When you grow up in that kind of atmosphere around the clock, you feel cared for. If there wasn't any food in our refrigerator, I could walk into one of our neighbor's apartments and open their refrigerator to find something to eat.

Growing up with everyone being so close and neighborly, living as one village community essentially, would play a big role in my life. I drew upon this core foundation for housing years later for creating the village community concept to help house our neighbors in need who are experiencing homelessness, which is now called Father Joe's Villages. I simply created the same kind of caring, neighborly community feel I knew from my own experiences.

Whenever I talk about the fact that everyone is our neighbor, I can't help but think of Abraham. I am an Abraham fanatic. I love scriptures around Abraham. A great power Abraham had was that he knew God's name. When God appeared and spoke to Abraham, Abraham asked God who he should say sent him. Abraham asked to know God's name, and "I Am" was the response. No one knew God's name before Abraham.

In knowing God's name, Abraham accepted responsibility, because once you know someone's name, you can't say, "I don't care because I don't know them." When you know someone's name, that means you know them. You're connected. They can't be a stranger any longer. Knowing someone's name is powerful because it creates responsibility. Once you know someone's name, you have a responsibility to them. They are your neighbor. We are responsible for each other. "Love thy neighbor as yourself." I think God knows what He's talking about and it's our responsibility to demonstrate that commandment in our lives. Whether it's when someone is living in a ten-apartment building in the Bronx or a housing community in downtown San Diego, or thinking more globally how we all live together on Earth, we are all connected because one person knows another person and so on. We are all connected when you think about it. We are all neighbors.

4.

St. Joseph's

My parish church growing up was St. Joseph's and it was an incredible building. But it's all torn down now. It stood three stories high on the corner of Bathgate Avenue and East 178th Street in the Bronx. It had a slanted rooftop and we played tag up there. It was thrilling because we'd slide down the roof to the edge that had a huge drop and have to stop ourselves before falling off. I don't know if our priest knew we did that.

The church was very important to me as a young person. It was central in my youth and my early development. Our apartment was basically across the street and down a block from St. Joseph's, and that's where my brothers, sisters, and I did everything. We had a group called CYO, Catholic Youth Organization. We used to do crafts and play games. My brothers and I played sports with CYO—football, basketball, baseball—and we played against other churches. It was at St. Joseph's where I was able to join the Boy Scouts. My sisters were very active, too, as they were all part of the Sea Cadets and participated in its full-size marching band.

We had pool tables in the youth room. It was the first place I got to play pool, which wasn't common for kids at that time because the only other place you could shoot pool then was at the bars. I also managed the youth newsletter and shared news on all the parish happenings and different groups within the church. Back in those days, I printed the newsletter on a mimeograph machine. I published it monthly. I liked being involved in church life.

It was through activities at our church that I was empowered with junior leadership. I was able to be a leader in scouting and coaching sports, and even be in charge of the newsletter. I experienced the opportunity to be a leader at a young age and have responsibilities, and I know that's why it has always been important to me to empower others. I really enjoyed being part of St. Joseph's and I took full advantage of being involved in everything I could. My siblings did, too. St. Joseph's was an active parish community and the Carroll kids were involved in every aspect. It was a home away from home for us. Also, we went all through Catholic schooling. We attended a Catholic primary school, most of us attended Catholic high school, and I went to a Catholic college. So we were very, very Catholic.

5.

Goody-Goody Joey Carroll

I was trusted as a teenager to have keys to everything at church. I was given more keys than a pastor or parish priest would have now. Because I was always doing good things, I became known as a goody-goody. No one would ever think I was doing anything other than good stuff. I mean, if I pulled you out of the school line and hit you, you would get in trouble. "Joey Carroll could do no wrong" was how people thought of me. There was no way anyone would ever think I'd do anything other than the right and good thing, which was true most of the time. I was so involved in everything at church and trusted by the adults that it was common for everyone to think I'd become a priest. But then people said it so much as I got older, I rebelled against the idea for a bit because I don't like people telling me what to do.

The truth is that when I was young, I did think about being a priest. It was there, on my mind. When I was a boy, I thought I was going to be one of three things when

I grew up: a Boy Scout executive, a mathematician, or a priest. Priest finally won out because you get to count the collection, so you can still be a mathematician, and I could still be a Scout Chaplain if I became a priest. And so all three things I wanted to do could be done in one.

6.

Naughty in the Neighborhood

The neighborhood police station was next to St. Joseph's. As teenagers, we'd go into the police station garage at night and steal the cop cars. We'd drive around the block and leave the cars elsewhere so when the cops came back on duty, their cars were gone. Yes, we did some bad things.

Another bad thing we did was steal baptismal certificates so we could go drinking. At the time in New York, everyone got a draft card when they turned eighteen, which was the legal drinking age. But because ours was such an Irish-Catholic neighborhood, a baptismal certificate would be accepted to prove your age, as it's basically a birth certificate. We were mischievous. I'd distract Father Joyce with a conversation and my friends would sneak in and steal a stack of baptismal certificates so we could prove we were eighteen to go drinking. So, baptismal certificates were the racket we had going at the time.

This was during Vietnam War times and every American

male eighteen years of age and over was drafted back in those days. So on your eighteenth birthday, you had to file to get your draft card. The system was that you got a notice to go down and take your medical exam, and then you'd get one token. The token meant you passed the medical. You're in the Army now. Don't expect to go home. Next thing you'd be off to Fort Dix.

After my medical exam, I didn't get a token. I was too handicapped to get drafted for war. I was designated 1-Y, which to me meant I was one "yellow" (a coward). I'd tell people I wasn't worthy for the draft so much so that I was put behind women and children. Even then I had bad legs. I didn't know the Army was going to deny me. I was willing to go be of service to my country. I thought I was okay. My legs told a different story.

7.

At the Copacabana

At eighteen years of age in New York at that time, you could get drafted into the Army and you could drink alcohol. For our proms, we'd go to the nightclubs to dance and drink booze and stay out all night long. But when I came out to California in my early twenties and was in the seminary meeting guys from the West Coast, they'd talk about graduating high school and how great their prom was at Disneyland. That sounded strange to me. Disneyland is great and all, but for prom? For this New York guy, Disneyland didn't sound like a fun rite of passage, since on our prom nights we went to Paradise Club and the Copacabana and stayed out well into the early morning.

Our proms in New York were always held on a Saturday night, which meant we were out until early Sunday morning—and Catholics go to church every Sunday morning, including after prom night. The churches in downtown New York had a solid plan for prom weekends. They knew hundreds of us were in the city celebrating and we needed to attend Sunday morning Mass. Back then, Mass was never held Sunday nights like now. But the churches in New York would have Mass on prom weekends at midnight, one o'clock, two o'clock, three o'clock, and four o'clock, since they knew we weren't getting up in the morning to go to Mass after being up all night. So, we'd go downtown nightclubbing for prom. Then, we'd go to one of these churches at two or three in the morning for Mass, take the subway home, and sleep through the next day because we'd already gone to Mass. We were much more conscious of church then than you can imagine. It didn't matter what was going on in our lives, Sunday we went to Mass no matter what.

8.

Shabbos Goy

There were a lot of Jewish people in our neighborhood. I was a Shabbos goy. That means I was a gentile, a non-Jew, called a goy, who would do work for the Jewish community during their Sabbath, their holy day of prayer, which is also referred to as Shabbat and Shabbos. The Jewish holy day of prayer starts at nightfall on Friday and lasts until nightfall on Saturday. According to Jewish law, Jews are prohibited from doing any work during their holy Sabbath day.

Now, turning on the gas and the lights in their homes, that's work. Cooking a meal, that's work. They couldn't do any of this from Friday night to Saturday night. They needed people to help inside their homes as they observed their holy day. That's what I did. I had a business where I'd go to Jewish homes in my neighborhood on Friday night and for ten cents a house, I'd turn on the gas and turn on the lights after it got dark. I'd do other jobs they needed done, too. I'd go down three blocks and do this building after building for each Jewish home. I did this for years. They trusted me.

My friends had newspaper routes at that time. They delivered the paper seven days a week. Now, we're talking New York. They weren't riding a bike from house to house. They were walking up and down the streets, and up to the fifth and sixth floor of every building, delivering the paper. They worked their butts off every day to make the same money I was making working Friday nights. I was a Shabbos goy. I didn't want a seven-day-a-week job. I wanted a one-day-a-week job.

There were three synagogues in our neighborhood, too. Ten males were needed to conduct Friday night services; women didn't count at that time. The males didn't have to be Jews. So another aspect of how I earned money was attending services for them. My friends and I would play games out in front of a synagogue and if they were short a male, they'd ask us to participate. So, for a quarter I would sit in their synagogue, with a yarmulke on, and listen to them pray in Hebrew. With three synagogues close by, I could get two in on a given Friday night.

When someone dies in a Jewish family, they have what they call shiva. They sit shiva. For a period of a week, it is their custom to mourn their family member and they aren't supposed to do anything during that time. They weren't allowed to go out shopping, so if they needed food or to get the paper—anything—I'd do it for them. I was their Shabbos goy. I was a big part of the Jewish community growing up.

This connection with the Jewish community continued throughout my life. In fact, when St. Vincent de Paul Center opened, one of the first groups to organize and commit to serving meals to our homeless neighbors on a regular basis was Congregation Beth Israel. It's been serving meals every Sunday since 1987. I have always respected my Jewish neighbors.

9.

Entrepreneurial Spirit

I've always had an entrepreneurial spirit. It's just how I am. There's always a way to create opportunities to earn money. When I was growing up, we didn't have money to buy anything extra or do special things, so I figured out how to earn it for myself to help my family and get the things I wanted. If you're willing to do the work, there's always a way to earn money.

I sold Christmas trees for the Boy Scouts. I sold Christmas cards for the high school. I sold chance books of raffle tickets for the church. That's how I got most things I wanted. I worked for it. I was really good at selling raffle tickets for church or school fundraisers. They'd always have a prize you could earn by selling tickets, and I'd always earn it because I'd figure out ways to sell more tickets than anyone else. I loved electric trains and one year that was the big prize. I was determined to win and I did. And guess where the best place was to sell chance books of raffle tickets if you're a kid? At the bars! Little Joey Carroll would just walk into the bar—kids could go into bars at that time—and next thing you know, I sold all my tickets. Other kids didn't think to sell in the bars. I did. I figured out how to sell a lot of tickets in one place and earn the prize I wanted.

I was always wheeling and dealing. I never thought there was anything stopping me. If there was something I wanted, I figured out how to get it by earning it.

The day I graduated high school, I rented my own apartment. I was seventeen and moved into my own place directly below my family's apartment. It was the same size. They were all in one apartment, all nine of them, and I was by myself, but my door was always open to everyone.

My place was a popular hangout and was where all the young people wanted to be on the weekends to party. I had a fully stocked bar. It was the best bar in town and the system was on Friday night, my brothers and sisters, the younger ones, could use my apartment for a party night and I'd be a chaperone. I was trusted to be a chaperone for teenagers just a few years younger than I was. On Saturday night, I'd have a party with the older crowd. Then on Sunday, my brothers and sisters would come in and clean the house. That was our deal. There were fourteen beds in the apartment, so if you got drunk and didn't want to go home to your parents, you had a place to stay. I was already sheltering people as a teenager.

But I had rules. I have never liked filthy language and

everyone knew they couldn't talk that way at my place. They also knew they couldn't tell dirty stories. Imagine, these are eighteen- to twenty-one-year-old guys and I'm telling them no cussing, no smoking, no dirty stories. I was a teenager and had all these rules.

And I ran it like a business. It wasn't a free-for-all. I had a price list for booze and everything in the refrigerator had a price tag. If you wanted a beer, you'd open the refrigerator and there was a price tag on each one. You had to pay. If you wanted whiskey or scotch, I had it all listed out and you had to pay for each drink. That was the only way I could afford to keep the supply. Best bar with best booze with best prices. If you wanted to enjoy the place, you had to contribute.

From the time I was eighteen until twenty-two, I mainly worked full time as a teller in a bank during the week. I liked working around money. It was math and I always liked mathematics. I didn't like working in the summer, so I usually quit my jobs for that season. That was vacation time for me to hang out. Then, after summer, I'd go back to work as a teller or get another job. I fixed laundry machines for a while. There were a lot of launders in the Bronx and that kept me busy. I usually worked multiple jobs, like my parents did. I've had a job since I was eight years old. I've always liked working and being busy.

10.

My Cross to Bear

I've been crippled my whole life. When people see me now in my wheelchair, having had both feet amputated, they think it's a new thing. But I've been dealing with leg and hip issues forever. Someone came for a visit recently who knew me from growing up; "How are your legs?" was the first thing he asked. Everyone who knew me then, knew me to be crippled. Being crippled is a main theme in my life. I didn't let it hold me back. I just figured out ways to do things. I had physical limitations, but I wasn't limited.

My first major surgery was when I was eighteen. My knees were such a problem that I would just be walking and my kneecap would pop out. It's not supposed to do that. So, I had surgery to adjust my kneecap. They took it off, shifted it, and tightened it into place. I remember distinctly thinking at eighteen, no more football for me. And since all the guys played football at the time, "Why did God do this to me?" was a momentary thought.

But that thought came to me at about the same time I realized lying next to me in another hospital bed was a guy my same age who was in a full body cast. He had been born with a curved spine; the only way they knew to fix it was to not let it grow, and the way they did that was keep him in a cast until eighteen—the age his body would stop growing. So, there I was lying in bed with a bad knee and feeling sorry for myself for a moment, while this other guy my same age was so excited to be getting out of his body cast for the first time to be able to learn to walk. It was a real awakening for me to know I had nothing to complain about. I realized then that there's always someone else who has it worse than me. I learned in that moment to be thankful for what God provided me. Others have it worse than me. I never complain.

Sometimes people will feel sorry for me and say I have every right to be complaining about all the things that have gone wrong in my life. I say, "No. I am thankful. I lost half my legs. Other people lost their whole legs. I am lucky."

From the ages of eighteen to fifty-three, I had knee surgeries every three years. Even when they amputated my right foot and then eventually my left, those experiences were not horrible for me. They were necessary.

My absolute worst experience happened when I was fifteen. I will never forget that day. I jumped off the bus that was taking me home from school. However I landed, it was wrong, and my knee popped out once I hit the sidewalk.

The pain was excruciating. The only way to pop it back into place was to get off of it, but I was three blocks from home. I had to get home, so I had to push myself along the sidewalk, practically crawling, for those three blocks. The whole way, people wanted to help me, but they couldn't, because I knew what I needed to do. When I got home, I crawled up the stairs and into a chair to pop my knee back into place. The pain was unbearable. I will never forget crawling along the sidewalk for three blocks. That was a horrible day for me.

As a boy, I sometimes used my knees to get out of things. Since I had a loose kneecap, I used to pop it out to stay out of school. If I didn't want to go to school that day for whatever reason, I would pop it out, let it get swollen, and say, "Mom, I can't go to school today. My knee is bothering me." She'd see it was red and swollen, and let me stay home. Then sometime during the day, when it was too late for school but early enough for me to be able to go out and play, I'd pop it back in and say, "Look, Mom, it's better!" And off to play with my friends I'd go when they got home from school.

Even though we were really poor, my parents made sure we had medical insurance. I remember when I was a boy, the insurance salesman came to our home every Monday. My mom would pay him each week for our family's insurance premium. She'd pay ten cents for some of us and twenty-five cents for the teenagers. That was a lot of money for us each week. I have always made sure to have medical insurance. It's always been a big expense for me. But I needed it because of all my surgeries. You can still see the knee surgery scars on my amputated legs. I am a history of orthopedics.

Through all my injuries and constant physical pain throughout the years, and even the stroke I had recently, you'd never know by the way I behave if I am in pain. People notice this about me. I don't complain. It's just always been part of my life. I never let it get me. I never let anything get me down. This has been my reality since I was a boy. Being crippled wasn't going away. I decided to accept it for what it was—especially after the day I had to crawl home from the bus stop. Being crippled wasn't going to beat me.

We all have things we experience in life that are difficult. It's our attitude toward our challenges, our pain, and our suffering that makes a difference in our lives and for those around us. I was taught as a kid in Catholic school that we are to offer our pain to join with Jesus's pain on the cross, and that made it valuable for me. When I joined my life's suffering with Jesus, who died on a cross for the sins of the world, I was raised to a whole new level of understanding about my own pain. My suffering was one with Jesus as He suffered on the cross. Therefore, what I was experiencing was raised to His level. My bad legs are tied into Jesus's suffering, so I'm with Jesus in the moment He's on the cross. That raises it to a much higher level that I can bear.

11.

Boy Scout for Life

I joined the Boy Scouts when I was twelve years old. To this day, being a Boy Scout is one of my life's greatest honors. Scouting helped make me who I am today. The values instilled in me through being a Boy Scout have been part of every phase of my life. They are part of me. The Boy Scout motto is "Be prepared" and the slogan is "Do a good deed daily." Preparation and goodness every day. Yes, that made sense to me.

There are twelve principles in Boy Scouts that we are to live up to, known as the Scout Law. "A Scout is trustworthy, loyal, helpful, friendly, courteous, kind, obedient, cheerful, thrifty, brave, clean, and reverent." I lived these principles. I really bought into it as a way of living life. I have always felt good being a Boy Scout. The Scout Oath is, "On my honor I will do my best to do my duty to God and my country and to obey the Scout Law; to help others at all times; to keep myself physically strong, mentally awake, and morally straight." I think there's value in scouting for everyone and that's why I liked being a Boy Scout leader, so I could help others experience the same goodness for themselves—to be stewards of goodness to others.

I never made it to Eagle Scout, though. Back then, some of the merit badges we were required to earn to achieve Eagle Scout included physical things I just couldn't do. And in those days, there wasn't much forgiveness for physical limitations, not just in Boy Scouts, but in society. It wasn't as it is now. Back then, if someone was in wheelchair, for example, there just weren't opportunities for them to be out and about. They'd be confined at home—in one place. There wasn't consideration then for any alternative. But now I am in a wheelchair and I can go wherever I want and do about 90 percent of the things I want to do. There aren't that many things I miss out on.

While it would have been great to have been able to achieve my Eagle Scout, I did achieve the highest ranking I could get to at that time with all things considered by reaching Life Scout.

12.

Best Camper

In scouting, some of my favorite activities were camping and being at camps, as well as going on special trips like to jamborees. But I first was introduced to attending camp by way of Camp Choate, an all-boys summer camp in Wallingford, Connecticut. Well, it was actually Saint Andrews Camp run by Choate School, but we Carroll brothers always called it "Camp Choate." My mom had found out about the opportunity for boys like us from lower income homes to attend. One year, she applied for my oldest brother, and when Jack came back from camp full of stories of how much fun he had, the rest of us wanted to attend, too, and followed in his footsteps.

We attended camp every summer of grade school. Over a period of fifteen years, one or more of the Carroll boys was there. Once you attended Camp Choate for five years, you were recognized as "Best Camper." It's closed down now, but when it was open, it had a bunch of plaques on the wall—an honor roll of names of everyone who achieved

Best Camper status. All our names were on the wall: Jack Carroll, Jim Carroll, Joe Carroll, and Tom Carroll.

We learned early that it was a different world up there for us. We were poor kids from the Bronx and the high school leaders were mostly these filthy rich kids from wealthy families— like the Kennedy's wealthy—who lived very different lives from us. My brothers and I had never really been anywhere else and these kids were flying to Europe for vacations. There were also other camper kids like us, and kids from all walks of life and all nationalities.

Camp Choate was classic for its storytelling. The high school leaders would tell joke stories to scare campers. And they did. Like the story about the "Red Glow," the name of a man who kidnapped campers. He would just hang out in the woods around the camp and we'd hear about how he'd taken other campers and they were never heard of again.

Well, as kids when we first heard this story, it scared us so much we wouldn't want to go outside at night. Then, let's say a kid got sick at camp and had to go home early. We campers didn't know he was picked up by his parents; we just found out he was gone. This was gold for the counselors, because they'd be able to reinforce the Red Glow story. We'd all be terrified.

Eventually, we found out it wasn't real and knew the routine, that Red Glow wasn't real, and then we became part of reinforcing the story to other campers. You weren't supposed let on to the new, younger campers. It was like a rite of passage.

There were other stories told, ones that weren't scary, and we learned a lot. We got to experience life in the open, in nature, unlike living in the Bronx. I liked being at camp those summers and my brothers did, too. Years later, there was a reunion of all the counselors. My brothers drove up there and got to see the camp, including all our names on the wall as Best Campers. We have great memories from those summers.

13.

One-Way Ticket to California

I loved growing up in New York. I have great memories there. But New York winters were really hard for me since I had severe arthritis. It usually took me one to two hours just to get out of bed in the morning, because I had to warm up my body to get it moving.

One November when I was twenty-two years old, I received a postcard from a friend who was living in California. It had a picture of the beach and sunshine. He wrote that it was always sunny and warm where he lived. November in New York looked opposite of the postcard picture. I finally decided I had enough of the cold. I wanted to be in sunshine and warmth.

I remember going upstairs to my family's apartment in the morning when everyone was getting ready for work and telling them I was leaving for California and was saying goodbye. They all said, "What are you talking about?"

"I'm going to go to California this afternoon," I told them.

They just thought I was talking crazy. But when they got home from work that night, I was gone. I had bought a one-way ticket to California. It was only one-way because that's all the money I had at the time. I could only afford to get there.

I arrived in Los Angeles with fifty bucks in my pocket and made my way toward Santa Barbara. I looked in the newspaper for a place to stay. Shorty Taylor was looking for a roommate. He said I could stay with him for thirty days until I found a job, and didn't have to pay rent that first month. I stayed with him for a few months, and then got my own apartment in the same building after I got a job in a supermarket and had myself established.

14.

The Reluctant Seminarian

One day after work, I was sitting on a bench waiting for my friend outside of his apartment building. That's when I met a priest named Father Roughan. He had dropped off another priest at the doctor's office across the street. Father Roughan had been walking up and down the street saying his prayers. When he walked by me, I said, "Hi, Father," and we ended up talking for a while. Next thing you know, I was touring the rectory, enrolled in the seminary, and part of St. Joseph's Parish. It happened quickly.

When I entered St. John's Seminary, I told no one back home. For the first two decades of my life, everyone told me I'd be a priest. I told them no way. I don't like people telling me what to do or who I am. I ran from it. But it found me. God knew. They all knew. Then, I knew.

Those first two years in the seminary, I didn't tell my family I was actually there. I had all my mail go to my old address. My former landlord would bring my mail to me and I never let on to my family. Then, one day I wrote to my mom and told her. She wrote back and said she knew the whole time. Moms always know.

When I first went in the seminary, I was a reluctant seminarian. My attitude was that it's a calling from God. I didn't want it. Since God was basically dragging me in, my attitude was that God had to do all the work. This lack of personal responsibility was reflected in my grades. I had a 2.51 GPA, which wasn't good if I wanted to graduate from college.

That is also what contributed to me being kicked out. I wasn't really showing much effort. I was being a lazy seminarian. I did the minimal amount of everything. To graduate from college, you had to have a GPA of 2.5 or better, so a 2.51 GPA was just skimming by. The powers that be didn't like this because I wasn't demonstrating a real desire to be there, so they didn't accept me into the graduate program. I was out.

Eventually, things changed within me. My desire became that I really wanted to be a priest. I woke up to it being my calling, not just God's calling. I felt a responsibility for my choice in being called. That's when my entire attitude changed. It was my choice. I wanted back in. I wanted to be a priest. I was willing to do the work. I took my education seriously. My attitude was reflected in my involvement and in my grades. Years later, when I graduated from graduate school, I finished with a 3.8 GPA. I had gone from being reluctant and lazy to being dedicated and serious. When my attitude changed, my results changed.

15.

Lone Scout

St. John's was the seminary for Los Angeles, so most of the guys were from LA County. I was the oldest guy in my seminary class. Normally, you went in at seventeen or eighteen, and I was twenty-four already—four or five years older than many of my classmates.

There were some seminarians who were coming in at seventeen, not quite eighteen. They hadn't become Eagle Scouts yet, but they still had time to meet the requirements. However, there was an issue of access. They were in the seminary and weren't allowed to go outside. I figured out how to help them. Through the Lone Scout program, I signed up as a Lone Scout Scoutmaster which enabled me to give every single scout merit badge and award there is and made it possible for some of the guys to receive their Eagle Scout Award.

16.

Pranksters

I like to have fun. I can be a bit of a prankster. When it was bedtime, we'd have lights out. And lights out meant it's lights out. All lights went off and it got dark. But when someone needed to study or finish a term paper, he had to find a place to hide to work. And since it was dark, he had to use a flashlight. There were four of us in a room. When someone would sneak back in at one or two in the morning after studying, I would arrange for there to be boxes of beads— the kind you'd use for crafts, thousands of them—rigged in his closet, so when he opened the closet door, thousands of beads would fall on the floor. So, I had a good side and a bad side; there were many stories like that. You might wonder why I wasn't thrown out of the seminary. Well, keep reading.

The guys were pranksters to me, too. It was ongoing for us all throughout our seminary years, and even long after it when we were ordained as priests. Whenever we got together, we often found some way to do funny things to each other. One time, the guys really got me during a trip to Lake Tahoe—in June. I had never been to Lake Tahoe and had no idea what to expect other than seeing pictures of people skiing up there. The guys all liked snow skiing in the winter and motorboating in the summer, and I liked gambling in casinos all year long, so Lake Tahoe sounded like a great place for us all.

Well, some of the guys arrived at Lake Tahoe before I did and decided to prank me. I got a call from my friend Terry Fleming before I left for the airport to catch my flight and he said, "Joe, we just wanted to warn you before you come, you better bring some warm clothes because Tahoe is pretty much snowed in right now. You need warm clothing." And he continues, "Oh, and they are in the middle of a strike on Pepsi up here. You can only go to Reno to get Pepsi, but Reno is snowed in right now so you can't get there. You better wear some warm clothes and bring your own Pepsi."

All of that sounded real to me, so I made sure I was prepared. Boy Scouts taught me to be prepared. When I got off the plane wearing warm clothes and a big winter coat carrying two six-packs of Pepsi, the guys were all just laughing. They got me. It was June and hot. It was swimming weather, not snow skiing weather. They knew I'd fall for it. That's the kind of friends we all were, always having good-hearted fun. Sam Cordileone was on that trip with us. He was still in the seminary at the time, and he is now the Archbishop of San Francisco. We called him Sam but his given name is Salvatore—now known as Archbishop

Cordileone.

We also all cared for each other. We were like family. One year while I was in the seminary, my classmates gave me a roundtrip ticket to New York. It was a surprise. Most of the guys were from around there, since St. John's is the seminary for LA County, so they could drive home for Christmas to be with their family. I wasn't going to see my family for Christmas because I couldn't afford to buy a ticket. I never really mentioned it other than when we were all talking about our plans. I was just planning on staying and working through the holiday.

One day after we had volunteered at Camarillo State Hospital (I have been helping the ill and mentally ill for a long time), we all went to see a movie. When it was over, they told me about the ticket. They took me directly to the airport and I got on a plane. They had it all planned, even packed my clothes. I had no time to call my family and tell them I was coming. So I just showed up, walked in, and said, "Hi, Mom. I'm home for Christmas. What are we eating?" That's the kind of guys they were. They were all just great guys. It was a good time in my life.

17.

Fleming Friendship

One of my close friends during that time was Terry Fleming. We are still good friends today. He is now a Monsignor in Los Angeles at St. Brendan Catholic Church. Over the years, we have traveled quite a bit together. We went to the World's Fair in Montreal. We went to New York. We went to Lichtenstein. I also heard his mother's last confession. She was dying and he asked me to do it. We still see each other quite a bit. He comes down to San Diego from Los Angeles about every six weeks. We've been friends for decades.

When we were in the seminary, my prayer time was nine o'clock. I'd often rest in my bed most evenings an hour and a half before then because by that time of the day I was in so much pain. My crippled legs have always been an issue. Terry would come to my room with milk and a cookie so I could take my medicine. I've never forgotten that.

Terry had a car when we were seminarians. He was always the chosen one. There were a few guys who were assigned to make trips into the city to go pick up things, medicine and stuff like that. It's almost like being a trustee. Terry's family lived in Oxnard and we were in Camarillo, which is only about ten miles away. We figured out a way to take advantage of that proximity. For instance, Irish people like to have a drink on St. Patrick's Day. But we were in the seminary. We weren't allowed to do that.

I soon figured out if I put a piece of paper in between my teeth, my gums would get red and irritated like I had an infection. That meant I needed an emergency trip to the dentist. Terry was the one who would drive me, so we'd stop by his family house and have a little drink.

The legal drinking age in California is twenty-one, so when you hit your twenty-first birthday, most people go out to have a drink. We were all in the seminary and obviously couldn't do that. Somehow we figured out how to smuggle alcohol in. And when we were in the elevator in the library building, which was also the same building the bookstore I managed was in, we could stop it between floors and have a little drink to celebrate a twenty-first birthday.

I was often skating between a little bit sinner and a little bit saint. I was usually somewhere in between, trying to see what I could get away with.

There were probably about one hundred guys in the seminary at that time. We were young men ultimately deciding if we wanted to become priests. Do I stay or do I go? That was the question. There are different steps you take and decisions you make while in the process, but the final decision you made to be a priest is the only one that counts.

But before I became a priest, I was kicked out of the seminary.

18.

Gold-Framed Baptismal Certificates

The main reason I was kicked out of seminary was because of how I managed our St. John's bookstore. The bookstore was focused on only selling books and there wasn't much profit in those book sales. When there were surplus funds, they were spent on student activities like movies for the student body, the art club, sports, and anything else that could be afforded with that money. Since it was a closed society, we didn't have access to many extras.

When I started managing the St. John's bookstore, I realized I had access to buying more than just books. I could buy almost anything at wholesale prices and sell to students at a discount. It was a fair-trade world and stores were all charging the same amount for everything. So, I figured out I could buy things students wanted—sneakers, sports equipment, typewriters, etc.—at a 40 percent wholesale discount and then offer products to students at a 20 percent discount. The school's bookstore made money and the student body saved money, which also meant students had more money to do other things since they weren't spending it on full retail-priced items. Everyone benefited from this wholesale system I created. When I was made manager of the bookstore, it made a little over $2,000 in profit per year. After I took it over, we annually made $180,000 in profit.

One of the reasons they told me I was voted out of being accepted into the graduate program at St. John's was because I was too far out of line when running the bookstore. For example, at the time, there was a book that had been published called The Dutch Catechism, which was a revised catechism that questioned some of the authority of the church. This book was forbidden in Los Angeles, and any store that sold it was no longer allowed to do business with the Catholic Church. That meant people couldn't buy the book anywhere. But I could get the book. I had access. I thought, "Hmmm, I can get something everybody wants and nobody could get." So, I got it and sold it at full retail price, no discounted pricing offered, and we made a lot of money on the deal. The powers that be at St. John's weren't happy about this when they found out. While I did a booming business for St. John's when I ran its bookstore, I was just too far outside of what they thought was acceptable.

A side business I created at St. John's was translating seminary textbooks from Latin to English. Many of our textbooks were in Latin. I didn't know Latin. So I paid a student who understood Latin well to translate the books into English. Then I sold translated copies to students. This was another booming business. There's always a way to make a buck.

Then the day came when they told me I was out. It was four days before graduation, and I was called in and told I wouldn't be moving on to theology, which meant I was being kicked out. They basically were telling me I needed to look for another career because they didn't want me anymore.

They had voted against me—that I shouldn't be a priest. They said I'd be the kind of guy who would sell gold-framed baptismal certificates. I shrugged, and said, "If it's a way to make money, what's wrong with that?"

Well, they didn't like that. I went around and met with each of the faculty and tried to talk them into taking me back. They again said "no" and I was out.

19.

Gap Year

I didn't leave the area. I lived in Carpinteria in a rented apartment on the beach for another year as I continued trying to convince St. John's to accept me back in for graduate school. St. John's is in Camarillo, which is about thirty miles from Carpinteria. When I was in the seminary for four years, I lived on campus at St. John's with the other seminarians. During those years, for holidays and summers, I had been able to get it set up to live in the rectory at St. Joseph's Parish in Carpinteria. Then, when I was no longer in the seminary, I couldn't live in the rectory and that's why I got an apartment at the beach; one of my nephews flew out to California and lived with me that year.

For work, I taught sixth grade at St. Joseph's School. Even though I couldn't live there, I had a great relationship with them and worked for them. At the time, St. Joseph's was in need of a sixth-grade teacher, as that class had been burning through teachers. No one was sticking. They believed I might be a good fit, thinking I wouldn't put up with anything from the students, and they were right. On the first day of class, I stood in front of my students and said, "Hi. I'm Mr. Carroll. If you ever do something that makes me send you to the principal's office, you will not be coming back to my class again."

And by the way, I had never taught school before. My only other teaching experience had been in scouting, so I used my Boy Scout skills with the sixth-graders. I basically learned how to do my job as I did it, which is similar to how I learned on the job when I took over St. Vincent de Paul years later.

20.

Second Chance Seminarian

When I was approaching the end of that year and still hearing "no" from St. John's about being accepted back in, I decided to call San Diego, since it was the next closest seminary. They took me immediately. They needed people.

I showed up at University of San Diego (USD) and they had me spend a year there. That way, they could get to know me, to see if we were compatible, and I got to know San Diego. The plan was, if all went well, I'd then get to choose where to go for graduate school. Since USD didn't have a theology graduate program, the San Diego Diocese sent seminarians to another place for graduate theological studies, like San Francisco, Ohio, Rome, and Washington, DC, which is where I went.

Being in San Diego for a year, I needed to do something because I hate to waste time. I decided to enroll in the graduate program and earn a Master's in Education degree. Because of that year teaching sixth grade at St. Joseph's, I learned a priest is an educator. A priest teaches on Sunday morning during the homily and classes for CCD

(Confraternity of Christian Doctrine). A parish priest oversees the parish school and decides on the school's budget. Understanding that being a priest meant I'd be very involved in education made me realize I wanted to get educated on education, and that's what I did by earning a Master's in Education.

I also was a substitute teacher at University High School, which was across the street from USD. When a priest took a day off, I was brought in to teach his class.

And all along the way, I was working side deals. If you asked guys when I was at USD for that one year, they'd tell you I ran a little bookstore on the side. If you ask priests from that period of time, they'd say they bought their Bibles and religious books from Joe Carroll. I had a book distribution business on the side.

And unlike at St. John's, I never got in trouble at USD for books. But I did get in trouble for throwing a party. Since the seminary is part of college life, I organized for us to have a party at the seminary with keg beer. It was like a fraternity party, but at the seminary. I don't think anyone had ever attempted that before. Yes, I got in trouble but I didn't get kicked out.

21.

Five-Finger Discount

After the year at USD, I went to seminary for four years in Washington, DC at Catholic University of America (CUA). Since Bishop Maher allowed us to choose where we wanted to go, I chose to go to our nation's capital because I would be able to visit my family a lot; they were just a few hours away on the train. This time, I had more freedom. We weren't as closed off as when I was at St. John's. I was allowed to go anywhere.

Soon enough, I had another booming business going. My brother-in-law in New York owned a wholesale electronics resale business. He'd buy a bunch of stuff in larger quantities at the manufacturer's wholesale price and then sell it in small quantities to small retail shops. He'd make his profit by selling items to shops for a markup that was still well below the retail price the shops would sell items for to retail customers. At the time, everything was fair trade. There were no discount stores. Everyone sold items at the same price. If one store sold a television for $500, it was

$500 in every store in America. No one could discount it. No one could put it on sale.

Let's say my brother-in-law bought the television for $250 and every retail store sold it for $500. If I could sell that same television for $400, I would be able to save people a lot of money and I'd make a lot of money. So, that's what I did. My brother-in-law would let me buy stuff from him at his wholesale cost—he didn't mark it up to me—and I was able to sell stuff to everyone in the seminary for way below retail pricing.

I could get anything he had at 40 percent discount. Well, priests and seminarians at school liked TV. They liked electric typewriters. I could offer them those items for way less than they'd pay at a retail store. There were hundreds of students at the college, so I could do a nice little business.

The only problem was, I had to get product from New York to DC, so I brought everything on the train. My brothers and sisters would drop me off at the train in New York with the products, and my seminarian friends met me at the train station in DC. All I had to do was sit on the train.

Yet, what I realized soon was that I was going to New York without any product. It was an empty train ride. At that time, DC didn't have any tax on liquor, so a bottle of scotch would be about three dollars cheaper in DC than New York. My family is Irish. The Irish like to drink. I quickly realized there was another opportunity. My seminary friends would drop me off at the train station with cases of liquor—

scotch, rye, bourbon, vodka. They would carry it on the train for me. My family would meet me in New York and carry it off. All I had to do was sit on the train.

One direction I was taking liquor, which was skirting the law. The other direction, I was taking typewriters, televisions, tape recorders—all kinds of goodies. It was quite the operation. I was saving everyone money in both directions because I could get them discounts on what they wanted. That's why everyone called it my five-finger-discount business—because they thought I had to be doing something shady to be getting such great prices. My friends would say, "Carroll, you're a shady character."

I never got in trouble for any of this because my buyers in the seminary were the priests. Who was buying TVs from me? Who was buying typewriters from me? The priests. And who are the people who vote yes or no for a seminarian to become a priest? The priests. I didn't get in trouble. I ran that five-finger-discount trading business the entire time I lived in Washington, DC. No one would believe this stuff. Then, I eventually became legit in wholesale resale with the St. Vincent de Paul Thrift Stores.

22.

Day by Day

While at Catholic University, a bunch of us wanted to go up to New York to see a play on Broadway. But the only one I could get us tickets for was Godspell, which was in an off-Broadway theatre at the time. The guys complained at first: "You got us tickets for a play no one has heard of."

We all went up to New York for the play and it was a really hot day. When we arrived at the theatre, the manager came outside and told us the air conditioning had broken down. He hoped we'd still stay and see the play. If we wanted a refund afterward, he'd give it to us. Well, we all fell in love with the play. It's that good. That is how it became one of our themes. It went on to be a hit touring production and eventually was on Broadway.

There's a song in Godspell called "Day by Day" that was really popular for a while. Its words are so great that I decided to use the song in my ordination. The songwriters created a wonderful prayer within the lyrics:

Day by day

Day by day

Oh Dear Lord

Three things I pray

To see thee more clearly

Love thee more dearly

Follow thee more nearly

Day by day

Imagine the power of these three simple things: See God more clearly. Love God more dearly. Follow God more nearly. Those words impacted me so much in my early life that I knew they had to be part of my ordination into the priesthood. God is not complicated. We don't have to make it complicated. God is with us day by day.

After graduating from Catholic University, I came back to California and decided to have my ordination in Carpinteria at St. Joseph's, instead of San Diego, since I had lived in Carpinteria or Camarillo most of my time on the West Coast. Even though I was part of the San Diego Diocese, I had arranged this with Bishop Maher; he understood my desire to be in Carpinteria for my ordination.

I decided to make a really big deal about my ordination. During that time, ordinations were usually held in large groups—thirty or forty men being ordained at the same time. That meant each man could only invite a few people to his ordination, because the church would reach capacity.

Since my ordination was going to be the biggest moment of my life, I wanted to be able to invite everyone I knew. I asked to have my own ordination, just me, and they allowed it.

My invitation had three designs on it: the Chi-Rho representing Christ, Abraham representing Abraham, and a chalice representing priesthood for me. Abraham said yes to God in faith. Christ said yes to God in accepting the crucifixion. I said yes to God in accepting priesthood—three things, a triad, like the Holy Trinity is three in one: Father, Son, and Holy Spirit.

In case you are unaware, an ordination is a ceremony in the Catholic Church where a person accepts a calling in the church from God to be a deacon, priest, or bishop. So for me, it's the priesthood. Through my ordination, I was agreeing to obey the Bishop in all things and I made three promises: I promised obedience. I promised celibacy. I promised to be faithful to the Gospel.

During the ceremony, the Bishop presents you with a chalice and he blesses your hands, because they will be set aside to say Mass so they're sacred. Our hands are sacred; they are doing the work of God's calling. Basically, an ordination is the transfer of priesthood. The Bishop lays hands on you, which transfers priesthood to you. And every priest in the church comes over and puts his hands on you to signify your priesthood as a unity of one. It's a oneness because Jesus is the only one true priest, and together we share in His priesthood.

Now, another reason my ordination was a little different than other ordinations was the news cameras. I felt it was a story worthy of being shared. I made a deal with a local TV station, KEY-T Channel 3 in Santa Barbara. I contacted them and said, "You're going to have an ordination here in town. It's an event that's never happened here before and may never take place again. I think it's a newsworthy story." They agreed and came, and aired the story on the nightly news.

I understood very early into my priesthood career that the ordination ceremony, that moment in a priest's life, is an important story to be told. It's a big deal and that decision impacts many lives. I don't think the church has ever done a good job of selling itself or sharing the important things it does for the community and the people who are part of it. I also understood early in my career that being on camera was important—it helped tell the story. Thus, I thought an ordination ceremony was a story that needed to be shared since most Catholics, let alone the public, never experience it. It was a chance for the community to know about an ordination taking place in their neighborhood.

For many Catholic parishes, a new priest just sort of shows up at the front door and starts. I think it's an important part of our religion that should be shared more openly. Nowadays, there are fewer guys being ordained into the priesthood and the ceremonies are smaller or more like mine where they have their own and invite everyone they know to be part of it.

A little while ago in San Diego, there was this young man in his mid-twenties from Pakistan making his vows as an Augustinian at St. Augustine High School. Because the gym at St. Augustine's where they normally do big services was being used at the time, they decided to do his ordination on the rooftop of one of their new buildings. Now, there were thousands of Saints men watching this young man step forward and give his life to God for all eternity. This is a ceremony you almost never see. It's special and uncommon. Why is this not being publicized—this eternal decision?

There is so much good being done within the Catholic Church. We need to make sure the news is focusing on the good stories. It is our responsibility within the church to make sure we are telling these stories, letting people know, and an ordination is a big deal. Some might say, "Oh, the press isn't interested in that kind of story." How do you know? Yes, it is. You have to lead them to the story. If they don't know, they can't be there. We need to be making a big deal of things and creating opportunities for people to have access to see and experience special Catholic events, like ordinations.

That's what I did. I made it a big deal. Buses of people came from Chino, from when I was a Deacon at St. Margaret Mary Church for a short time. Buses came from St. Brigid's in San Diego, as I was a Deacon there, too. I invited everyone. Most people would never get to see an ordination, so I tried to make mine as public as possible. My family flew out from New York and even Ireland. My dad had died by then, but my mom and all my brothers and sisters, and their spouses came, but not too many of their kids because a lot of them weren't born yet.

This was the biggest moment of my life; I wanted everyone there. I was becoming a priest.

Part of the ceremony is you lie down and people pray over you. I mean, you're lying down on the floor, people are praying over you, and you're really alone. And you say to yourself, "Do I really, really want to make this last step?"

I said yes. Everyone always said I would be a priest. I didn't like being told what to do. I didn't want them to be right when I was younger. But they were right. That was the day they could all say I told you so.

23.

Parish Life

To me, being a parish priest is the best job a priest can have. It's what I imagined I'd do for my whole priesthood—be part of a parish community and perhaps teach at the parish's school since my degree is in education. Yes, parish life to me is the best life for a priest because you get to participate in the fullness life has to offer with your parishioners.

Priests get to be present for all of life's most important events. As a priest, I have been there for all the big stuff. I've been present as people experience all their significant Catholic moments—the Seven Sacraments: Baptism, Penance (confession), Eucharist (Holy Communion), Confirmation, Anointing of the Sick, Marriage, and Holy Orders. For Catholics, these life moments are extraordinarily important, and I get to be there. It's incredible to me to have that privilege.

I mean, how many times does someone have their first Eucharist—their first ever Holy Communion—that significant moment in the Catholic faith? Once. It happens only one time and I get to be there. Your child gets baptized once. You confess for your first time only once. You get married once—well, that's my hope for people. And for all of those important life moments, I get to be there.

I have been able to experience life's significant moments with people, and to me that is a great honor. And in any given parish, there can be 1,000 or more people. A priest is present for most, if not all, of their important life moments.

So for me, every week I had exciting stuff happening. Life is full of celebrations and as a priest, I get to be there. Life is also full of challenges and changes, and I get to be there, too. I am there holding someone's hand as they are dying. I am there as someone releases their burdens in confession and as couples work through marriage matters.

For the big stuff and the everyday life stuff, as a parish priest, I've always felt like it's a privilege to be present with parishioners through it all. A parish priest is present regularly as people grow through life. I think it's a great life.

One misconception people have about the life of a priest is that all we really do is say Sunday Mass—like we have a lot of extra time on our hands. This is not the case at all. Priests work seven days per week. We are always on and our days are long. A typical day in the life of a priest includes morning Mass, then there are meetings and events, funerals to attend and confessions to hear, CCD classes to teach, youth groups to run, marriage counseling sessions to have, and more meetings to attend. That's just during the week; it is typical for our day to start at 7 a.m. and not finish until 9 or 10 p.m.

Our weekends include weddings and Mass, and other special events and gatherings. It was normal in the summer months for me to have multiple weddings on any given Saturday. Also, since I have always been involved in scouting, there'd be events to attend regularly throughout the year, including Eagle Scout Award ceremonies.

Priests go where they are needed. If parishioners are in the hospital, we visit with them. If families are in crisis, we visit with them. It's like we are on call all the time.

Also, at all three of the parishes I worked at, there were a lot of organizations and committees within them, and some people thought the priest should be at every one of their weekly or monthly meetings. I couldn't possibly attend every meeting. At one parish I worked at, there were over one hundred different organizations that met regularly. I couldn't attend anywhere close to all of those meetings. I also couldn't stay for the full length of any of them. It was just impossible. I didn't have that kind of time.

I learned to make it known, a rule really, that if I came into your meeting, the person in charge of the meeting would let me interrupt the meeting for few moments to say my two cents, and I'd leave. It had to be on my schedule, my timing, because I had multiple things going at any given time. This is the reality of many parish priests.

One time someone said to me, "Well, Father Joe, you need to come at the beginning because we can't disrupt the meeting." And I replied, "Okay, then don't expect to see me." I wasn't able to work my schedule around their meeting time and I couldn't sit through a half-hour meeting just to say hello when the meeting agenda warranted it.

It was crazy to me that some people didn't get this. I think it's an important thing for people to realize even now. Priests are busy and needed at multiple places at the same time quite often. As much as we may like to be present with everyone and attend everything, we just can't. So yes, if you are the one running a meeting, you can certainly pause it and let the priest do his bit so he can get on his way; he may have three other meetings to drop by that night or have youth group to lead, or something else.

One time, I didn't drop into a meeting and some people took it personally, like their "thing" was not important to me. No, that was not the case. A fellow parishioner was in critical need and I had to rush to the hospital to be with him; that took priority above all other things.

That's why it was always important for me to have a great secretary to help be a buffer or the voice of my calendar, keeping things prioritized. If someone called in with a need for me that was immediate and urgent, which meant my attendance at something else would need to be postponed or cancelled, I had someone working for me who could handle alerting them as to why I could no longer be there. I have always prioritized my presence to be with people first above all else. Most "business" matters can wait. Someone in crisis can't. People have always been what's mattered to me most.

24.

Pepsi Priest

I always enjoyed having meals with parishioners. Yet, as much as each gathering was enjoyable, I usually couldn't stay for hours and hours visiting. Like I said, in any given evening, I'd have a few places to be. During the year, I'd have meals with parishioners a couple times per week.

Then in summer, our parish housekeeper went on vacation for three or four weeks. That meant we didn't have home-cooked meals in the rectory, so I'd let everyone in the parish know during Mass on Sunday that my calendar was open to having dinners with them. They'd call in to the rectory office and my secretary would organize a schedule for me to have dinner at a different home every night. It was fabulous—great food and great company. My secretary would always let each household know my time frame, when I'd arrive and how long I could stay. This made things clear. She also had a great way of making sure I wasn't served the same meal multiple nights in a row.

I remember one summer in particular when I was mentoring the San Diego seminarians, they went to dinners with me. I had always enjoyed mentorship, so helping be a leader with the seminarians was a natural fit for me. They liked it because I was young, closer to their ages than the older priests. They would invite me along to things they wanted to do as their buffer, like if I was with them, it was okay to be out a bit longer or whatever.

These summer dinners helped set the example of how important it was to share meals with parishioners while also being clear about setting expectations. We'd arrive for dinner and visit, then be off by 7 p.m. to get back to the parish to lead youth group or a meeting, or do something else. Archbishop Cordileone was in the seminary at this time and he came to a few dinners with me, along with some of the other guys. I was showing them the ropes of the whole deal of priesthood. Priests have to eat. These dinners were important. I am still connected with many of those seminarians.

It was during this time I also learned to make sure everyone knew, before my arrival for a meal in their home, that I drank Pepsi and only Pepsi. For one thing, I really did only drink Pepsi. Yet more so, setting this standard was really all about my protection because I was able to see how alcohol could become a problem if I wasn't careful. I am Irish, and it's customary for the Irish to drink whiskey or scotch. Thus, when going to someone's home for dinner, the assumption was to serve a cocktail or at Christmas to gift a bottle of booze. Imagine if fifty parishioners gift fifty bottles of whiskey—that's a lot of booze sitting around. That could become a problem. I didn't want it to be a problem for me.

What really drove it home for me was one time I was talking with some teens about addictions and drugs, encouraging them to not smoke marijuana, which was their drug of choice and illegal across the board at that time. One of them said, "Well, Father Joe, you choose to drink alcohol and that can be an addiction." That really hit me. He was right. I was choosing to drink alcohol which they were seeing as a problem, especially since some of them had bad experiences with alcohol in their homes with alcoholic family members. I wanted to lead by example. It felt important to me. To this day, I remember that moment clearly. I couldn't tell them to not do something I was doing in a similar way, so I stopped drinking booze.

I became known as the Pepsi Priest. There's no need ever trying to serve me something else. It's Pepsi and only Pepsi, and always has been. Well, I had to switch to Diet Pepsi some years back because I have diabetes and my body couldn't handle all the sugar in regular Pepsi. Nowadays, every time I go to the hospital for something, the doctors always tell me I need to drink a lot of liquids. I hear liquids, not "drink more water," so I do. I drink Pepsi. Pepsi is maybe 99 percent water plus caffeine and color, so I am following their orders.

25.

Signature Stamp

Upon graduating from seminary, my first parish assignment was to Our Lady of Grace Parish (OLG) in El Cajon, California—which is in San Diego County. Bishop Maher, who was in charge of the Diocese of San Diego, was responsible for designating us to our assignments. As I vowed in my ordination into priesthood, I was obedient to his leadership. This included obeying his orders whenever he sent me to a different parish and when he assigned me to be in charge of St. Vincent de Paul years later.

While I was at OLG, a new rectory was built on church property. In my apartment area within the rectory, the furniture I was using had originally been donated from a parish family. It was used furniture and I liked it because it was comfortable for me. One day when I had hurt my back and was lying down in my bedroom, I heard a few people talking in my living room, saying, "Well, this will have to go. That will have to go."

I got up, went in there, and asked what was going on. I was introduced to an interior designer who was apparently brought in to redecorate my living area. They wanted to get rid of my couch because it was too big and old looking. I said, "No. I like that couch because I can lie down on it." That's when they told me I was not supposed to lie on a couch. Shocked, I said, "Excuse me. Did I miss something?"

That's when I was told the Bishop was coming for a visit and OLG's Pastor wanted there to be nice furniture throughout the rectory in every room when he arrived. I was annoyed. "So for me to live here, I had to take old, used furniture. And now the Bishop's coming just to have a look and we have to get all new furniture. This doesn't make sense." I didn't let up; I told them the Bishop can just take over my apartment if it's being designed for him.

Yes, I was annoyed and I reacted. I even called down to the school and had the eighth-grade boys come up to move me lock, stock, and barrel into the garage. All in one day, that very day, I was moved out of the rectory apartment and into the garage. Naturally, the Pastor didn't like this. "We can't have you in the garage. The Bishop will go crazy!"

I didn't care. I had my place as I liked it for me. That was it. I had a bit of a temper about it.

Besides this interior design quick change for the Bishop's visit, I found the Pastor to be difficult to get to do different things. This annoyed me so I found a workaround to his procrastination. I had found out that Mac, who was the old bookkeeper, had the Pastor's rubber stamp signature. Mac handled the bills at the end of the week; he would just stamp the Pastor's signature onto the checks. I thought, "Mac has the signature stamp to sign checks in his desk drawer." And I knew the Pastor hated to confront other priests, meaning if you do something, he won't challenge you. My mind was spinning. There's a blank check and a signature stamp in Mac's drawer—hmmm. So, I went on a few spending sprees courtesy of the Pastor's stamped signature.

Now, what I was buying on these sprees wasn't what other people would buy with a blank check. For example, I think every CCD teacher should have a new Bible, but the Pastor didn't agree. He was too cheap to spend the money. I didn't like that. So, I went out and bought forty bibles for all the teachers with a check bearing his signature. And just as I had banked on, he never said anything to me about it.

26.

Youth Ministry

In my time as a parish priest, I was assigned to three different churches in San Diego County. Our Lady of Grace was first, which we always called Our Lady of Money among us priests then, because it was quite a wealthy parish with a large property in El Cajon, east of San Diego. St. Pius X in Chula Vista was next, south of San Diego, and then I was at St. Rita's in central, southeast San Diego. I got to experience three different parishes with three different demographics of parishioners.

While each parish is a unique experience, what was common among them all for me was being involved in youth ministry and scouting, Boy Scouts and Girl Scouts. Normally, youth ministry involvement is for young priests who are just getting started; they eventually grow out of it into other areas of parish life. But being involved with helping empower youth has been part of my entire life, mainly because it is what I personally experienced.

I had been a Boy Scout starting at the age of twelve and moved up the ranks into junior leadership as a teenager and then scout leader at eighteen. I also had the opportunity to be a youth leader at my church as I grew from my boyhood into my teens. It has always made sense to me to empower youth the same way I was empowered, not only because I experienced it, but because I grew from it. The responsibilities I had in youth leadership helped me learn about people and figuring out what they needed; it helped me work with groups and get things done. I thrived, and I also just naturally stepped up to take charge and lead.

Because of how it benefited me and how I saw others grow when they were empowered as leaders, I have always trusted junior leadership. But you have to let them lead. They can't lead if you don't empower them with opportunities to be in charge, to lead groups, to earn their way, and to help inspire and train others under them to do the same.

So, that is what I did at each parish. I made sure we had active scouting programs and youth groups with junior leadership empowered, running meetings, and being in charge. And I made sure it was fun. They had meeting and fundraising time, and they had fun time.

I made sure we were doing things kids and teens like to do. Youth ministry isn't a hard concept to figure out. To be a youth minister, you have to accept kids as kids and do things kids want to do.

I remember at one parish, to help get more kids attending

youth group I organized a Disneyland trip. We let everyone know it was twenty dollars to go to Disneyland, with ticket and transportation included; this was back in the 1980s. We had 500 kids sign up. People were shocked. They couldn't believe that many kids were interested in going. Really? It's Disneyland. Of course kids wanted to go. I made sure we did fun things kids like to do. Period.

Years after this, when I was at St. Vincent de Paul, we opened a teen center called Toussaint to provide housing and schooling for homeless teenagers in need. When leadership was discussing activities for the teens to do, I wanted to make sure we did fun things for them. Some people opposed my ideas because they said many of the teens had adult experiences by then and wouldn't want to do those things. And I said, "So what, they are still kids." They may have had adult experiences, but they haven't had fifteen-year-old experiences yet; they were still seeking that without knowing it. Some of the kids had never been swimming in a pool or gone snowboarding, or attended camp or gone fishing. I wanted them to experience those things.

27.

Movie Mania

Some kids had never been inside a movie theater. Going to the theater and seeing a new movie on the big screen has always been a fun thing for me and that is why to this day whenever a big movie comes out, I will rent an entire movie theater the night before its release and give tickets to youth and their families. This is a great treat for people who can't afford to go to the movies. It was a luxury thing for me when I was a kid growing up poor in the Bronx. So, when I was able, I started booking out theaters when special movies came out.

I even did this when the new Star Wars movie came out in 2019. As a way of saying thank you to people who visit me, assist me, and bring me lunches, I wanted to do something special for them and their children and grandchildren. Being able to see Star Wars: The Rise of Skywalker the night before it premiered to the public was special. No one else could get tickets, but I had an entire theater booked the night before for a special viewing. It was terrific. I actually did this same thing for all the Harry Potter movies in past years as well. It makes me happy to know kids could brag the next day to their friends that they got to see the movie before everyone else. That's the fun stuff.

28.

Fundraisers for Fun

One thing all youth groups and scouting troops always need is money. They need funds to be able to do activities—to do fun things. I was always coming up with ways to help youth and their families have opportunities to raise money so they could earn their way to participate. We did a lot of fundraising to do fun things, and I always tried to make raising money fun.

A popular fundraiser I started while at St. Rita's Parish was selling loaves of bread after Mass on the first Sunday of every month. We offered bread from Dudley's Bakery, a popular bakery that's about fifty miles outside of San Diego, in a rural mountain town called Santa Ysabel. Its bread was very popular and at that time, you could only get it if you drove out there. So, we sold Dudley's bread and the youth programs made a lot of money. I'd help increase sales at every Mass by announcing how much I liked potato bread. Sure enough, after each Mass a few families would buy loaves of potato bread and give them to me. Then, before the next Mass, I'd give those loaves back to the kids to resell so they could make even more money. I wanted them to benefit. I was always willing to help them earn.

At each church, I always made sure we had seasonal fundraisers going on, selling what people wanted and needed. During Christmastime, we'd sell wreaths after Mass—real greenery. On Mother's Day at every parish, we'd have all of the mothers stand up during Mass to be acknowledged and we'd give each of them a single red rose. Then at the end of Mass, we'd announce that the youth group was selling roses outside. I'd say something to the men like, "If you want to show your wife how wonderful she is, you'll buy the other eleven roses to make it a complete dozen." This was a popular fundraiser, too.

I was always a wheeler and dealer, but there was purpose to it.

29.

Viva Las Vegas

One of the most memorable trips I took while I was a parish priest was the one and only time I did a combined trip with a Boy Scout troop and parish youth group. The road trip was to drive through Las Vegas to the Grand Canyon and back through Las Vegas. During the trip, I realized there's a difference between organizing and running a Boy Scout trip and a parish youth group trip that included boys and girls.

For one thing, we needed more time in the morning to get everyone out the door and on the road. For Boy Scout trips, it was a quick wake up and get going morning routine. For this trip, the first few mornings, I'd be waiting and waiting by the vans for the girls to come outside. What was the holdup? "Oh Father Joe, we can't leave yet. The girls are still in the bathroom fixing their hair." They're what? What do you mean they're fixing their hair? Well, of course they're fixing their hair. I had sisters; I remembered this. I just didn't factor in this extra time in the mornings. I was impatient at first because I wasn't used to it, since all my Boy Scout trips were we're up and out, but I adjusted and learned.

It's hard to believe all of what happened on that one trip. It taught me that no matter how detailed the plan, be prepared to expect that anything can and will happen. For example, we were in Las Vegas staying in a parish hall. That is what we normally did on all trips, stayed at churches for free accommodations. The phone rang at about two o'clock in the morning. I got up and answered it in the parish hall, wondering who would be calling me at that hour. Well, it was one of the dads calling from San Diego. "Hi, Father Joe. How's the trip going?"

I said, "Ummm, it's going great. But I don't think you called me at two o'clock in the morning to ask me that. What's going on?"

He then asked me, "Is my son still with you?"

I said, "Yeah, I can see him right now. He's right outside the window of the office I'm standing in."

The dad said, "Really? He just called me from the sheriff's office."

What? Sure enough, a few of the boys had stuffed their sleeping bags and snuck out to explore Las Vegas in the middle of the night. I felt horrible and a bit embarrassed to have this dad calling me about his son sneaking out without me knowing.

Well, Las Vegas was very strict about kids who were underage out past curfew and it was even worse if the kids were smoking marijuana, which was illegal at that time. So this group of boys was in major trouble—minors out late smoking marijuana. To make matters worse, when the police officer questioned them, they wouldn't give their names. They refused. So, the officer threw the book at them by arresting them on the spot and making them stay overnight at the station. They eventually got their names out of them and called their parents in San Diego.

I went to court the next day and the judge berated me. "What kind of leader are you that this could go on? How could you let these kids get away with this? You weren't watching them." It was bad, and I took it.

When the judge was done letting me know how awful of a leader I was, he said, "Release them to the Father." He meant to me, Father Joe. But the court clerk thought he meant to their fathers, their dads, who were all back in San Diego. I didn't know that and found myself waiting for a long time for them to get released. When I finally asked what was taking so long, when would the kids be released to me, the person at the desk was confused. I was told they were waiting for their fathers to arrive from San Diego. I was extremely annoyed and said I am the Father they were supposed to be released to. Soon enough, they confirmed this with the judge, but it was too late; their dads were already driving to Las Vegas to get them. We didn't have mobile phones back then, so there was no way to intercept them. As you can imagine, those dads were not happy when they arrived.

On this same trip, one of the girls woke up one morning and her sleeping bag was all wet with blood. She had started her period. I had never experienced this before on a trip and in my mind, I was thinking, "What am I supposed to do? I didn't get this training in the seminary." Yes, I had sisters, but their personal matters just weren't anything I had any awareness of when growing up.

As it turned out, I didn't have to do anything. The other girls stepped in and took care of her. It was so amazing for me to see how they all just rallied together to help their friend because that girl had no idea what was going on with her body. Apparently, her mother never told her about what to expect because she didn't want to explain about sex. We had female leaders on the trip, too, of course, so it was just handled. This was my first trip with girls and I learned a lot about them, including being prepared for what they'd need with supplies that are different than what boys need.

30.

Poker Priest

Then there's another thing that happened on this trip; I couldn't make all of this up if you paid me. We had it arranged for one of the girls to stay with her grandparents, who just happened to be staying at Caesar's Palace on the Las Vegas Strip at the same time we were there. This made sense to me to let her see her grandparents and sleep in their nice hotel room versus on the floor in the parish hall. So we dropped her off at the hotel, and she went running inside to go be with her grandparents.

None of us knew her grandmother had died in the hotel about two hours before this. Next thing you know, they called the parish to say she wanted to come back to be with the group; she was traumatized and wanted to be with her friends. They had to track us down through our van driver's CB radio to let us know this—remember, no mobile phones. We were still close by because our vanload of kids had all stayed near Caesar's. The kids had free time to go off in groups to explore the Strip, and I played poker. I love gambling and hello, we were in Las Vegas, so I gambled.

Of course, I don't wear my priest attire while sitting at a poker table. I had been at one particular table for a bit, along with a woman who was telling some raunchy jokes that made everyone else laugh. I had just been minding my own business playing poker, not really saying much. Then, right after she tells another off-color joke, one of the youth group kids walks up to the table and says, "Father Joe, we have to leave." So now everybody at the table looks at me with eyebrows raised, realizing I am a priest who had been sitting there listening to the woman's really dirty jokes. No, this was not my finest moment.

I got up to meet all the kids and leaders outside by the van. If you've been to Las Vegas, you know there's a water fountain in front of Caesar's Palace. On this day, there were tons of bubbling soap suds in this massive fountain. Yes, you can guess it. The kids had poured soap in the water. I had let them loose in Vegas and they made Caesar's Palace bubble.

31.

Loitering Leader

While I was with a vanload of youth group kids on this Las Vegas Strip adventure day, the Boy Scout group went to the Grand Canyon in the other vehicles with the scout leaders. They all hiked down into the canyon, stayed the night, and then hiked back up—meeting all of us there so everyone could see the Grand Canyon.

On this day it was really hot, well over one hundred degrees, and someone in another hiking group had given one of the scout leaders an ice-cold beer. He didn't drink it then, but did take it and put it in his bag. Then, when we got back to the parish hall, it was his rotation to have a break. That is how it worked on those long trips; every leader had designated time off to do what they wanted. He decided to stay and relax at the parish hall while the rest of us went off to do something else. At some point, he went outside and laid on the grass in front of the parish hall to drink his beer. Soon enough, the cops showed up and arrested him for loitering because here was this man, lying on the grass drinking a beer. He looked like he was up to no good and none of us who knew him were there at the time to affirm his story.

I remember this one trip so clearly because it was the trip I learned the most on, especially about rolling with the punches—because some things you just can't control or even plan for. Truly, how much can happen during a week-long trip? If it can happen, it will happen.

32.

Bobble Head

I got a call the other day from two men, brothers Gilbert and Elliot Cotto. They were part of my Boy Scout troop in the Bronx back in the late 1950s and early 1960s. They would have been about fourteen or fifteen years old at the time and I was eighteen. We didn't have any other adults leading the troop, so I became the scout leader at just eighteen. They decided to call me to let me know their mother had recently died at age ninety-five, and she apparently had my bobblehead in her bed when she passed. Yes, there was a Father Joe bobblehead made some years ago that was given to donors as a fundraising incentive for our yearly Thanksgiving Day 5K run. Around Mrs. Cotto's room, there were photos from when I gave Gilbert and Elliot their Eagle Scout Awards in 1960—pictures of me with their whole family. She had appreciated the impact scouting had on her sons; those moments captured in pictures, and apparently the Father Joe bobblehead, were some of her life treasures.

Her sons were also two of the boys from my troop back then in the Bronx who I had selected to meet astronaut John Glenn. I had become known among the scouting council for having one of the biggest troops in the region. My scouts were from all walks of life, and were achieving a lot of badges and awards. So whenever there was a parade or special event, they'd call me to participate and they'd often want me to suggest some scouts to be featured. When I was contacted about John Glenn being at the Waldorf Astoria in New York City to recognize Eagle Scouts, the Cotto brothers were two of the scouts I selected. They got to meet John Glenn and take photos; it was a big deal. Their mom was so proud. Those photos were on her bedroom wall, too.

It had been many decades since I had last communicated with Gilbert and Elliot. They told me not only about their mom, but also how important scouting was to them personally. When they were teenagers, many of their friends who did not join scouting ended up joining gangs and some even got arrested. They wanted me to know their lives were better because of scouting, especially during those years when they could have taken a different path with some of their peers. They let me know that through the years, their parents would always give thanks to God for scouting and their leader Mr. Carroll—that's what they called me back then. As I am nearing my eightieth birthday, it makes me feel good to know I have had a positive impact on people's lives and it stretches back to when I was just a teenager.

The Cotto brothers felt compelled to let me know

about their mother the day they discovered the Father Joe bobblehead in her bed—and thought about their experiences sixty years prior. We had some laughs on that call because they remembered I didn't let anyone off the hook then. While I liked making things enjoyable, I took leadership seriously and was a strict scout leader. I was only a few years old than them, but I was firm; I didn't let anyone get away with not upholding the standards of being a Boy Scout.

My own family would agree with this. You can ask my brother-in-law, Nick. My sister Peggy ended up marrying a guy named Nick who had been in my Boy Scout troop when he was a teenager. One time, I had organized for my troop to go on a camping trip out of town for a week during the summer. Early on in the trip, this guy and another kid disobeyed me and insulted me. I wasn't having any of that. I put them on a bus and sent them home, just like that. Well, the parents of one of the kids had planned a trip for themselves, as they expected their boy to be gone for a week. They had to cancel their vacation. They were not happy with me at first. His mom even said I was a thief because I robbed them of their vacation and they weren't able to get a refund. But that was not my problem. It wasn't my fault their son was disrespectful to his leader. The lesson needed to be learned. Then, years go by and my sister ended up marrying him. We laugh about it now.

In my conversation with the Cotto brothers, one Boy Scout trip we talked about that they remembered well was the

1960 National Boy Scout Jamboree in Colorado Springs, Colorado. That was my first of a handful of jamborees I attended over the years. It was also the year of the Boy Scout Golden Jubilee that celebrated fifty years of Boy Scouting. To attend that jamboree was a really big deal. That year, there were eight buses from our area that drove to Colorado Springs to attend. It was a big adventure for all of us, especially since many of us from the Bronx had never been that far west in our lives.

Talking about that trip and that time of my life in scouting brought back a lot of memories, many of which I hadn't thought of for years. It all reminded me how much scouting has always been a central part of who I am. I am proud to be a Boy Scout for life. Like my family and my faith, scouting has been tremendously important to me and influenced many of my life decisions.

33.

Shining in Scouting

Scouting is a great example of experiencing the opportunity for growth in others. I have seen it through countless people I've known through the years, and I've experienced it personally. I became a Boy Scout because it was an opportunity offered to me at my church when I was growing up. I loved every aspect of it. I earned every medal, badge, and award I was able to earn at that time, with my physical limitations being a factor for the ones I wasn't able to achieve. I was able to earn my way up the ranks to being a youth leader, and that led to me being a scout leader at age eighteen. Those leadership experiences led me to become a Lone Scout Scoutmaster in seminary to help other seminarians have the opportunity to earn medals, badges, and awards. And all that led to me continuing my work with scouting when I became a priest through today. I made sure to have scouting troops at each parish I was assigned to, for boys and girls. I became the San Diego Scouting Chaplain and then Boy Scout National Catholic Chaplain.

Because scouting offered me many wonderful opportunities for growth, I have always made it a priority to attend every scouting ceremony I am invited to whenever possible. Even to this day, with having some limitations with my health and always requiring assistance with transportation being in a wheelchair, my presence at scouting events is important to me. If they earn it, I do my best to honor that achievement by being there. Presence is important.

I remember at one parish, it was customary to always make a big deal when a boy made his Eagle Scout Award; there was a Mass that was well attended. That's great, but I realized we weren't making as big deal of it when the girls earned their awards, and that didn't make sense to me. Earning the Gold Award in Girl Scouts is equivalent to earning the Eagle Award in Boy Scouts, and I have always thought if they earn it, we need to recognize it.

Actually, it has always been my thought that if anyone in a parish was achieving something extraordinary, it needed to be acknowledged. A parish is like one big family, so gathering to honor and recognize exceptional things earned and achieved is important. And that is what we started doing. We'd have a Mass that recognized achievements earned by our Girl Scouts and Boy Scouts, and we made a big deal of it. Every pew was filled with people there for Mass to honor them. When our youth have the opportunity to achieve big things and they choose to do the work needed, gathering to celebrate and honor those achievements is important.

34.

The Gift of Universality

There are so many wonderful opportunities available in scouting, but one thing it has provided me is universality. Through scouting, I've been able to experience the oneness of being united with other scouts from different cultures and nationalities, and from different faiths.

You have to understand, my entire world growing up was centered around the Catholic church. Most everything I did was at my church. That meant most of the people I spent time with outside of school were Catholic, since all the sports and activities I was involved with were at our parish, St. Joseph's, even scouting. Being in Boy Scouts offered me the opportunity to experience different things. Growing up in the Bronx, there were many different ethnicities and religions on the same block or within blocks of each other. Scouting opened the door for me to be welcomed into their churches and places of worship in a different way. When I became a youth scouting leader, I started getting invited to help lead meetings and trainings for other troops, most of which were not at Catholic churches like mine.

For example, when I was about fifteen, I became a scout trainer. I started training other scouts in other troops on a bunch of things, including knot tying, which is a big skill taught in scouting. Word got around and eventually I was being asked to teach knot tying at most of the Boy Scout troops in the Bronx—Jewish troops, Protestant troops, Methodist troops—everyone was asking me to help. I was in high demand. I have always enjoyed helping out and teaching others, so I said yes to every request.

What those experiences at other churches and synagogues taught me was that Jews were okay. Protestants were okay. Methodists were okay. Everyone was okay. Teaching knot tying taught me about how similar we all are in many ways. Scouting helped me have opportunities to interact with people of different faiths. It also taught me about how Jesus lived. He was friends with everyone. Yes, I am Catholic. It's my faith and how I live. In living out my faith, I do my best to be and live as close to how Jesus lived as possible—and that means doing my best to be respectful of everyone. When Jesus said love your neighbors as yourself, He meant everyone. Jesus didn't say love only people who believe like you, look like you, live like you. Everyone. Everyone is our neighbor.

35.

Jamborees

I briefly mentioned Boy Scout jamborees earlier, but they deserve more focus, since attending them is one of the ways to experience the universality of scouting on a bigger scale. Every four years, there's a National Boy Scout Jamboree that lasts for ten days, with about 40,000 scouts attending from all over the US. From the 1970s through 2010, national jamborees were held at Fort A.P. Hill in Bowling Green, Virginia. In recent years, they've been held at Summit Bechtel National Scout Reserve in West Virginia.

The World Scout Jamboree occurs every four years, too, and is held in different countries, similar to the way the Olympics occur every four years in different countries. I've had the pleasure of attending national and world jamborees; they are spectacular events with everyone gathering in unity as scouts.

The National Boy Scout Jamborees I have been to were attended only by boys in scouting. But the World Scout

Jamborees I attended had girls, too, because in most other countries scouting isn't separated by gender. Eventually, the US followed suit, with Boys Scouts of America changing to Scouting of America and offering gender-combined troops.

Back when I attended jamborees, the deal was that there was a special jamboree troop from San Diego organized specifically for the event. To qualify to attend, you had to be a certain age and rank in scouting. Those who met the criteria would apply through the San Diego Scouting Council; it determined who was accepted and formed the jamboree troop.

When I was a parish priest, and even years later when I was running St. Vincent de Paul, I encouraged scouts to apply. The experience of attending a jamboree is that significant and I wanted scouts to have it if they could. But these trips weren't cheap. It cost a few thousand dollars per person to attend. Not many families could outright afford it, so we did a lot of fundraising for those jamboree trips.

36.

Hot Dog and Pepsi Stands

In the late 1970s and early 1980s, a great fundraiser we did was selling hot dogs and cups of Pepsi outside of grocery stores on the weekends. Those hot dog and Pepsi stands were how a number of families paid for their sons to attend jamborees, and of course the scouts did the work to earn their way. I encouraged it. If they wanted to go on the trip, they needed to work for it. This scouting fundraising concept of hot dog and Pepsi stands happened for quite a few years before some wholesale warehouse stores started offering hot dogs and sodas in front of their stores. It worked for us, and it works for them.

Looking back, I was always fundraising for Boy Scout stuff and coming up with different ways for us to earn money. There's always a way to make money if you're willing to work for it. My parish troops and jamboree troops knew the deal. Do the work to earn the money to do the fun stuff. And work is what we did. We worked at a book distribution warehouse tearing covers off books to be recycled. We earned money for each cover. We tore off a lot of covers. We did standard fundraisers things, too—bake sales, car washes, candy sales.

All the fundraising I did as a teen back in the Bronx for my first Boy Scout troop combined with the fundraising I did as a parish priest for our youth groups and scouting troops proved invaluable when I took up my biggest fundraising challenge. It was fundraising on a grander scale when I needed to raise millions of dollars for St. Vincent de Paul to build housing opportunities for our homeless neighbors in need.

37.

National Jamboree Chaplain

For one of the national jamboree trips I attended at Fort A.P. Hill, I was selected by the National Chaplain to be a chaplain for one of the camps. For this jamboree, San Diego Scouting Council wanted to send three troops. They were concerned they were not going to be able to get enough boys to apply. I said I'd sponsor one of the jamboree troops if they let me organize an all-Catholic troop. The council said if my troop was accepted as an official sanctioned troop by the national jamboree, they'd allow it. I applied and we were accepted.

It's important to note that only a certain amount of troops are accepted as sanctioned jamboree troops, for both national and world trips. Being sanctioned means you get to stay on the grounds within the official jamboree. Other troops that applied and didn't get accepted as sanctioned could still attend the jamboree daily, but they had to stay outside of the official jamboree grounds. That is what happened for one of the world jamborees in Canada. The troop from San Diego didn't get sanctioned as an official jamboree troop and while it attended every day, it couldn't set up camp within the jamboree grounds. The scouts went back and forth.

All in all, these jamboree trips, as sanctioned troops or not, are incredible experiences—youth gathering from all over to participate in activities together, unified with the principles of scouting. For many, these were life-changing opportunities, as some of these kids had never been outside their own city. It was only through scouting that they could have the opportunity to take a three-week trip, traveling to a new place and meeting people from all over the country and even the world. It opened their eyes to a bigger world—meeting new people and having new experiences. I am sure if you ask any scout who has attended a jamboree, he will tell you how that experience impacted his life in a positive way.

38.

Media Mass

While being a chaplain at the national jamboree at Fort A.P. Hill, I decided to do a jamboree-wide Mass on Sunday morning. Normally, we never did large Masses at jamborees for two reasons. First was logistics. Since there were 40,000 scouts camping on the jamboree grounds, there were about thirty or forty campsites spread out over miles of land. It made sense to have smaller campsite Masses with one or two campsites combined, which meant they could have one to two hundred kids and leaders at Mass. Second, at that time, Catholic leaders were encouraging things to be smaller. Instead of Mass being a big experience, we wanted people to feel closer to it.

For this jamboree, I had a different idea. I wanted to do something really big and bold.

Normally at jamborees, the LDS church had a jamboree-wide service and it was always attended by thousands of Mormons. Well, I was feeling a little extra competitive that year, thinking if the Mormons could do it, the Catholics could do it, too. But of course I wanted to take it one step further than just having big attendance; I wanted to have media coverage.

Jamborees usually get a fair amount of publicity because having 40,000 scouts communing in one place is a big news story. I wanted them to feature our Mass on television. I contacted some of the local news stations and pitched our story. I spiced it up a bit more because I arranged for our Mass to also include the official presentation of the St. George Medal to the Pope's ambassador, who'd agreed to attend and accept the medal humbly on behalf of the Holy Father. Now this was really special, bigger than life. Sure enough, the news stations agreed to come and film our newsworthy event.

Then, since I had the Pope's ambassador agreeing to attend, that meant the local bishops all decided to attend, too, because if the Pope was going to be getting an award, they had to be there. They couldn't not show up.

So, I had the Pope's ambassador and ten bishops all in full vestment attending a Catholic Mass and the news media showing up for this big Catholic news story. I had this thing pumped up to be a really big deal. I just needed everyone to show up.

On Sunday, Mass was supposed to start at nine in the morning. At quarter to nine there were no more than twenty scouts in attendance. I am not kidding. Twenty! There were multiple news crews with cameras already there; a news helicopter circling overhead; ten bishops and the Pope's ambassador in full vestments, in the middle of the summer; and there were only twenty scouts. I'm thinking to myself, "You have got to be kidding me. This is turning out to be a flop, an absolute failure of an idea."

And just when I was having the slightest doubt that this idea was not so great, all of a sudden like a scene from a movie, scouts started arriving by the hundreds. I looked up to see crowds of scouts cresting the ridge, walking down the hill toward us from every direction. Mass was being said in an outdoor amphitheater-type place that was sunken down, like a bowl. So when I was down near the altar at the bottom looking up, all I could see were scouts in uniforms descending down into the amphitheater for Mass, hundreds after hundreds after hundreds. What a sight to see.

Many of the scouts and leaders who attended Mass that morning had to walk four or five miles to get there from their campsite. But I don't think anyone was disappointed. It was a special Mass for everyone. Afterward, scouts took photos with the bishops. Most of the scouts had brought their jamboree souvenir booklets with them for the bishops to autograph. The news crews got their story, and we got a lot of publicity. So all in all it served its purpose.

It was a total success! We ended up having over 7,000 people in attendance for that Mass. Catholics did end up having a bigger gathering than Mormons at a jamboree. Yes, I have a little competitive streak in me. But it's healthy, I think. It drives me to get results and having the news share good Catholic stories has always mattered to me.

39.

Oh Come All Ye Faithful

Speaking of big moments, one year I was the Chaplain at the World Jamboree in Sydney, Australia, and I said Mass for scouts from all over the world. As you can imagine, at an event like this, there are people in attendance who don't speak English. If you're Catholic, you can follow along with the priest because most of the Mass is said the same way in any language.

When it came to music during Mass, I wanted to do something special. One song I knew we could all sing together was "Oh Come All Ye Faithful," because no matter what language you sing it in, the melody is the same and most Catholics around the world know that song. So, that's what we did. Thousands of scouts from all over the world singing together, "Oh come all ye faithful, joyful and triumphant." We had probably fifty different languages going at the same time with scouts singing in their native language. Everyone singing in unison was an amazing experience of oneness, as Catholics and scouts.

40.

Cheerful Scout

In thinking through all the scouting trips I took over the years, one of the main things I've focused on is having fun. I don't think anyone will ever accuse me of being boring or dull. I like to make things fun and enjoyable. I have always leaned toward being spontaneous rather than rigid. When traveling on scouting trips, there would be a plan for where we were going and what we were doing along the way, but I'd often change that plan spontaneously based on what the scouts wanted to do. Prior to the trip, I'd have it all mapped out—an outline for each day's agenda and a plan for where we'd stay each night along the way. Yet once we were on the road, I would make changes based on what I heard the boys talking about.

For example, one bus trip we were on was going through Yellowstone National Park. I was sitting in the front of the bus and could hear what the boys were talking all about. I heard one boy say, "I hope we get to go fishing." Well, I hadn't planned for us to go fishing. I immediately opened up the AAA travel books I always brought along with me on every trip and read that fishing was allowed in Yellowstone and no permit was required at that time for people eighteen and under. Done deal! I reworked our agenda so we'd be able to go fishing. And that's what we did. We all went fishing.

One time we were on a bus trip across the country and I heard one of the boys talking about how much he liked NASCAR. I didn't have that on our trip agenda. Soon enough, I figured out a way to make it work. I was able to make some arrangements and rerouted one of our days so we could all attend a NASCAR race. While on the bus with the roadmap in hand, I'd think to myself, "Okay, we can go to Notre Dame then head over to the Indianapolis Speedway. We'll pick up McDonald's along the way because I heard someone say he'd never eaten at McDonald's." I made it work. The kids loved it.

For every trip, I'd tell parents ahead of time to expect our daily schedule to change and be okay with that. Since we usually took these bus trips in the summer, some parents would want to surprise us on the road since it was their vacation time, too. I was normally okay with that, but only if they were okay with the fact that we may not be where we planned to be as written on the agenda. It was important for me to make sure parents were flexible with the plan being changed while on the trip. Everyone was usually good about this.

If you ask me which of the twelve scouting principles best describes me—trustworthy, loyal, helpful, friendly, courteous, kind, obedient, cheerful, thrifty, brave, clean, or reverent—I'd say cheerful. I am a cheerful scout, and I am a cheerful person. Being cheerful is a characteristic that really speaks to your disposition. For me, it was not something I developed. Being cheerful has always been part of me and scouting helped that grow. Even when I was being a strict scout leader, I was cheerful about it. We can follow the rules while having fun.

As a priest, I've visited with many people in the hospital in dire circumstances, and I always crack a joke when it's appropriate to help lighten things up. Imagine, I am there to say Last Rites to someone who is dying, and I crack a joke that makes everyone laugh. For that moment, I am able to ease their pain and get them laughing, even through their tears. It's part of the way I help people ease their burden. Now, someone else trying to crack a joke at that same time may come across as inappropriate, but not for me.

I have officiated a lot of weddings over the years and I like to tell a joke or funny story during every ceremony. The couple has no idea that when they are counseling with me in all of our premarital sessions, I am actually taking notes on the funny things they say about each other and the stories they share with me. Then, I bring out those notes during their wedding ceremony and have everyone laughing. The first wedding I ever officiated was my brother Tom's. I didn't hold back. I had a lot of funny stories to share during that one.

It's safe to say if I am speaking, I am most likely sharing a funny story or cracking a joke. My homilies during Mass usually include some sort of story or joke. Even when a subject matter is serious, I like to make it lighter with laughter.

Through the years, I have counseled with couples before they get married and through their marriage. When some of life's greatest challenges start coming into play, I do my best to lighten things up by getting them to focus on the aspects of each other they enjoy. One of the phrases I acquired while being part of Marriage Encounter for so many years is this: "God doesn't make junk." This is true with couples, and in all aspects of life when in relationships with others. It is God's will for us to see the goodness in each other.

When I took over St. Vincent de Paul with the mission to provide housing for people experiencing homelessness, I carried all of these aspects of my life experiences forward into that role.

Part 2

41.

St. Vincent de Paul

It was while I was at St. Rita's, my third parish assignment, when everything changed for me. I had been a parish priest for eight years by that time and was really in a groove, living the life God called me to live. I was involved with parishioners and scouts; everything was terrific. I had no intention of ever doing anything different. Yet, I'd soon discover God had another call on my life.

One day, I was in Bishop Maher's office having him sign certificates for an upcoming Boy Scout award ceremony. We had some scout leaders earning the Bronze Pelican Award and Saint George Award and the Bishop personally signed each award certificate. As I sat across from him at his desk, watching him sign the certificates, he paused, looked up, and said, "I'm naming you the head of St. Vincent de Paul tomorrow." Just like that, out of the blue.

I was stunned. That meant he was taking me out of parish life and changing everything for me. I was not happy about it at all. To me, being a parish priest is the best life. It's what I envisioned priesthood would be for me from the moment I knew I was meant to be a priest. To not be a parish priest was never a thought I'd considered. On top of that, I had zero experience working with people who live on the streets.

It didn't seem like the right fit. I was confused and asked him, "Why me? Of all of the priests in our diocese, all of the outstanding quality men you could choose from, why are you asking me to do this?"

He looked me straight in the eye and replied, "I asked a bunch of priests who they thought the biggest wheeler and dealer hustler was in our diocese, and your name was the only name on the list."

I told him I didn't want the job. I was not interested in being taken out of parish life. Now, it's important to point out how assignments worked at the time. When the Bishop told us he was giving us a new assignment, we were allowed to turn down his first assignment, but we had to take the second option, no questions asked. Remember, obedience to Bishop Maher was one of the things I vowed to do when I was ordained.

After telling him I didn't want the job at St. Vincent de Paul, Bishop Maher told me there was only one parish available for a new priest assignment and that was in Needles, California, a small city way out in the desert that's best known for logging the hottest temperatures in the state. After presenting option number two to me, the desert assignment, he grinned and asked, "Are you sure you want to turn me down for St. Vincent de Paul?"

Bishop Maher had me up against a wall. I didn't want to be in the desert. I liked living in San Diego. At that point, it wasn't a hard decision to make. I agreed to take over St. Vincent de Paul.

As intended, the next day Bishop Maher announced I was assigned to take over St. Vincent de Paul from Monsignor Topping, who had resigned and retired for health reasons. The transition started right away. I no longer had parish duties, yet I'd remain living in St. Rita's rectory as it was my home base. It would remain that way for about twenty years until I moved into the house I still live in on 16th Street, which is situated in the center of most of the buildings that are now known as Father Joe's Villages.

In taking over St. Vincent de Paul, Bishop Maher had one main project for me to do. I was tasked to build a homeless shelter on a city block of land we owned in downtown San Diego that was being used as a parking lot. The "wheeler and dealer hustler" part of the job was all about fundraising, because there was no designated budget in place at the time to build or even sustain the homeless shelter the land was purchased for. Since my scouting troops and youth groups always had a lot of money, thanks to fundraising, Bishop Maher figured I'd be able to raise what was needed. He assigned me the job and I was intent on doing it as expected; however, he never told me how to do it. He basically let me loose to figure it out, and that is exactly what I did. First, I had a lot to learn.

42.

Million Dollar Parking Lot

In the early days of being a priest in San Diego, the young clergy would get together a few times a year to have pizza and beer. We were young men at that time and liked to see each other and just talk, like guys do. One of our gatherings took place soon after I had been assigned to St. Vincent de Paul. We were all sitting around a rectory dining table eating and talking when one of the guys asked me what I was planning on doing about the shelter they wanted me to build downtown in place of the parking lot.

At that time in San Diego, east downtown wasn't built up with high-rises at all and the parking lot was next to a residential area. The original thought for that land was to build a few houses or a small shelter. But that didn't make sense to me. I grabbed a napkin that was on the dining table and drew out what I saw it to be. I pushed the napkin forward and said, "Here you go. This is what we're building."

I had drawn a rough sketch of the city block with a three-story building resembling what an apartment building looks like. My thinking was that we had this empty parking lot in downtown San Diego on land that was worth a million dollars, so it didn't make any sense to build a small place or just a few houses that would shelter ten to twenty people. That seemed like a waste of money to me. I thought we should build something bigger that would maximize the entire property so we could house a lot more people. I grew up in the Bronx where there was no wasted space.

Someone asked me, "What's a building like that going to cost?"

I didn't know much about construction, but I knew enough to know that you normally don't go above three stories, because once you do, you need all kinds of steel and that's way more expensive. I knew wood framing could go up to three floors high and that's why I drew it to be three stories. But what it would cost, I had no idea.

I responded, "I don't know. Three stories—one, two, three million dollars plus another half million to furnish it. So, it will cost about $3.5 million."

There was a priest there that night who said, "That is the dumbest idea I've ever heard. It's never going to happen." We argued a bit and he eventually said, "I have enough power in this diocese to stop you from doing it."

43.

Project Preaching Priest

Well, a few days go by after that gathering and I get a phone call from Monsignor Bolger, who was the Pastor of St. Mary Magdalene Church, the parish of the priest who said he'd stop me from doing it. Apparently, Monsignor Bolger was not happy about one of his priests boasting about stopping me and he called me up to say, "Joe, I want you to preach at my parish about your project."

Now, here's the thing. I honestly had no idea what he was talking about. I was racking my brain thinking, "what project?" You see, at that time, the shelter's building concept wasn't more than a conversation over dinner and a scribbled sketch on a napkin. It wasn't solid in my mind as an actual project yet. I wasn't thinking about it because I had just gotten the job.

I said to Monsignor Bolger, "Well, Bill, can you explain the project to me because I don't know what the heck you're talking about."

He said he heard about the shelter building from one of his priests, reminding me about the dinner discussion at the young clergy gathering a few nights before. He wanted to help. Oh right, that project!

With my memory refreshed and realizing an opportunity to start raising money had just fallen into my lap, I took Monsignor Bolger up on his offer to preach about the project at his parish. We set a date for the following Sunday and he set some expectations for me. He told me the most his parish had ever raised for a group outside of their own church was $5,000. He said if I could raise that amount, I'd have the people behind me believing in the project.

The Sunday I spoke at St. Mary Magdalene Church we raised $22,000. It was a total success.

The next thing I knew, pastors from other churches were calling me and asking me to come and talk to their church. I started preaching about the project at churches all over town. It was incredible. Everyone wanted to help.

44.

Mission Building

At that very first parish I visited, St. Mary Magdalene Church, one of the parishioners was a woman whose son, Mark Bucon, had just graduated from architectural school. He came to meet with me and said he wanted to donate his services to help design the shelter. I said, "That's great. But look, I need it done right away. I need a picture of the building this week."

Mark told me he couldn't get it done in just one week, but I insisted. I explained I was going out to meetings and had talks lined up at churches almost every Sunday. I needed to have something to show people so they could see what the shelter they were donating to help build was going to look like. I thought for a second and then said, "Make it look like a California mission."

And that's what he did. He created a rendering that was similar in design concept to the twenty-one missions in California, and covered the entire parking lot space as

I envisioned. We like to call Father Joe's Villages of St. Vincent de Paul the twenty-second California mission, unofficially of course.

From there, the project started creating more and more momentum. People wanted to give and were calling me to volunteer and be involved. The project had a life of its own. Interest was growing faster than I had things in place. When I visited churches those first few months, I didn't even have a donation envelope to hand out. I'd use their stewardship envelopes and wrote in St. Vincent de Paul on the donation line. Everything was grassroots, all starting from ground zero.

One day a fundraising luncheon was organized and we had the building rendering on display. Bishop Maher was there; it was the first time he saw the building concept. He pointed to it and said, "What's this?"

Things had happened quickly and I never talked to him about it. I said, "Well, that's the shelter you asked me to build." Thankfully, Bishop Maher kept letting me run with it.

All the while, I never had a long-term idea in mind about my involvement with St. Vincent de Paul. Honestly, I figured I'd build the shelter—do what I was assigned to do—then hand it off to another agency to run and go back to parish work. I thought it would be a short-term deal for me.

But God had a different plan. I was meant to stay and help it grow, never going back to parish life. And the more I got involved in the work, the more I understood the unique needs of people living on the street were greater than just housing. I knew I was meant to remain in my position after it was built and develop it—never handing it over to someone else to run.

45.

Learning Curve

When I took over St. Vincent de Paul, I started out with no funding, no programs, and no real understanding of the people I was serving. What I did have was a downtown warehouse thrift store, a city block with a parking lot, and a desire to learn and do my job well. For the first six to twelve months, I had a really steep learning curve.

Essentially, I had to learn about three key things quickly. I needed to learn how to be an effective fundraiser. I needed to learn about designing a building. I needed to learn about homelessness and sheltering people. And those three things were intertwined. I couldn't do one effectively without knowing about the other two.

To learn about fundraising, I enrolled in a program in Los Angeles that taught me about being a fundraiser. Working with my original thought, I knew I needed to raise at least $3.5 million. To do that, I knew I couldn't just rely on sending out letters with donation return envelopes or

implementing other parish-sized fundraiser ideas. I needed
to learn how to raise money on a much larger scale.

In my fundraising program, I learned how to write grants. I
had never written a grant request before or knew anything
about them. I learned about foundations and seeking
funding through foundation grants. I learned about how
there is government funding available to organizations like
us doing the work we were doing. I learned about seeking
funding with a broad-based approach to reach more people.
I also learned about the importance of creating unique
events that would appeal to people from all walks of life.

To learn about designing a building, I talked to everyone
I could about construction and materials—and politics. I
learned quickly how important it was for me to know what
was going on with city politics, because city leadership and
local ordinances impacted what we could and couldn't do.
I started educating myself on being a land developer in
downtown, which is ultimately what we became over time,
as we bought more land and buildings through the years.

To learn about sheltering people, I traveled around
the country touring other shelters to see how other
organizations and agencies were doing it. In that process,
I discovered what I liked and didn't like. For one thing, I
realized how important it was to me to make sure our shelter
was nice inside. I wanted it to feel like home to people who
stayed there, even if it was just for a short while. Most of
the shelters I toured at that time had open-room concepts

with cots or bunk beds in one big space. They had an institutional feel to them. I knew I didn't want to replicate the standard "three hots and a cot" concept of homeless shelters that was common at the time—meaning three hot meals and a cot to sleep on would solve the problem. I knew I wanted to do something different than what was being done, and that is ultimately what we did.

Learning about fundraising, building, and sheltering was essential for me to do my job. But what was most important to me was gaining a real understanding about the people I was meant to help shelter. You can't create solutions for something you don't understand. I didn't know what it meant to be homeless. I had a lot more to learn.

46.

The Lazy Scoutmaster

As I was learning, momentum for the project was picking up. I knew I needed help. I started by recruiting people I already knew from the parishes I had been part of. From hiring my first secretary and a new thrift store manager to volunteers and members of the board of directors, many of the people who were involved in the early stages were people I already had some sort of relationship with—from working together on projects at a parish, through scouting, or as parishioners. As everything grew and more help was needed, staff and volunteers branched out from there. Many roles in the beginning were filled by people who had been referred to me by those who were already employees or volunteers.

As the project received exposure, more people wanted to help and be part of it. It's incredible to me to think about how many people committed to being part of the work we were doing in those early stages who are still involved in some capacity to this day. This includes many monthly donors who have been faithfully contributing for decades.

I will say time and time again that I was just a catalyst to get everything going and lead it forward. It's people who have made all the difference. It was through the hard work and ongoing commitment of volunteers, donors, and employees of St. Vincent de Paul that we've been able to do what we've done and continue to do—helping impact lives in positive ways.

As my staff of employees and volunteers grew throughout the years, from just a few people to hundreds, I believe my leadership style remained consistent because it was something that was ingrained in me from when I was a teenager leading my Boy Scout troop. Based on a concept created by Robert Baden-Powell, who founded the international scouting movement, I learned the best scoutmasters are lazy scoutmasters. Basically, when you've effectively trained and empowered your scouts to be leaders within the troop, they run everything. Trusting junior leadership to do their jobs, the most effective scoutmasters can be lazy—guiding, teaching, inspiring, and answering questions, but not actually doing all of the work for their scouts.

As a youth scout leader, I liked this concept because it allowed me opportunities to be a leader while also educating and empowering other scouts to aspire to lead and grow into becoming leaders themselves. I experienced empowerment in action and it just stuck with me. In a scouting troop, there is a senior patrol leader who leads the patrol leaders who lead their patrols of scouts. There is internal leadership within a scouting troop just like there is internal leadership within a company or organization.

While I didn't have prior experience being a CEO or president of a company or organization, I had a lot of experience in leadership through scouting and I knew it was effective. I simply incorporated those ingrained principles into how St. Vincent de Paul was organized, and it worked. For me to be an effective CEO, I thought like a lazy scoutmaster.

In the beginning, I did a lot of the day-to-day tasks because I didn't have enough people in place to handle how fast things were happening. As I was able to hire more staff, I did what I knew worked for me in the past. I educated, empowered, and trusted people to do their jobs, and it worked. I've never micromanaged people. That doesn't work. I let people do what they've been brought in to do, and more often than not, they exceed expectations. No matter what work title I've had through the years, I have always led like a lazy scoutmaster.

47.

My Bathroom Office

My first office was within the St. Vincent de Paul Thrift Store on the corner of 16th and Market streets in downtown San Diego. The thrift store was basically a warehouse that had been converted to function as a retail store. When you walked into the store, there was a small office-sized room near the entrance. It had been used for storage and I changed it into an office that my secretary and I used at first. I soon realized I needed my own office to conduct meetings. There just so happened to be two bathrooms side-by-side next to the office, so I had the men's bathroom gutted and closed off, and made it into my personal office.

Nothing was fancy. I used what was available and made it work. We were all under one warehouse roof working within the thrift store. There wasn't a heater or air conditioning originally. If it was hot outside, it was hot inside. If it was cold outside, it was cold inside.

I eventually had a second level balcony area constructed for offices and meeting space that lined two walls of the thrift store. It became the space where volunteers helped with mailings and fundraising outreach. As I was able to hire staff, they worked up there. I worked from that thrift store office for many years. That property was eventually built up, years later, to be a high-rise of transitional housing apartments.

48.

Comic Book Inspiration

A few months after I got the job, I read a comic book about St. Vincent de Paul because I didn't really know anything about him. I knew he was the patron saint of the poor, but I didn't know much else. Yet, I wasn't interested in reading a big book about him. I just wanted a quick overview. A comic book was a perfect option. I learned about how St. Vincent de Paul had been a priest of privilege among the wealthy, but then was kidnapped and made to be a slave. In slavery, he lived among the poorest of people. When he was freed, he dedicated his life to helping the poor.

In helping the poor and homeless, he discovered many compassionate women wanted to help doing whatever was needed and never sought accolades or recognition. The group of women who helped St. Vincent de Paul would become known as the Ladies of Charity, which is actually a national organization. I knew immediately that is what we needed. By the end of my first year, the Ladies of Charity Auxiliary of St. Vincent de Paul was established in San

Diego. Women from all over the county joined.

From day one, the Ladies of Charity have done anything and everything you can imagine to help. I can remember back when the women would gather in the downtown thrift store to do our donation mailings. There wasn't enough space for all of them to work in the upstairs meeting area, so the women would sit at dining tables that were for sale within the thrift store to fold letters and stuff envelopes.

Years down the line, some of the women came to me and told me the national organization wanted to raise their dues and make sure each chapter was exclusively Catholic. Neither of these things worked for our group. The women didn't want to pay more money and they were from different faiths, including the newly elected president for that year, who was not Catholic. They wanted to branch off from the national organization and do their own thing. Since the whole idea of everything being done through St. Vincent de Paul was ecumenical, inclusive of all people and all faiths, it made sense and I said, "Sure, go ahead and do it."

They removed themselves from the national organization and voted to change their name to Ladies Guild. To this day, the Ladies Guild is an integral part of the volunteer work at St. Vincent de Paul. Volunteerism greatly contributes to the success of all that's been done, and the Ladies Guild has been part of it all in a major way, well before the first building was constructed.

49.

Peanut Butter Sandwiches

My introduction to serving food to people who were living on the street was by way of our daily peanut butter sandwich distribution from a side door of the thrift store. Every morning, people lined up around the building, mainly men, to receive a peanut butter sandwich. The system at the time was that the sandwiches were prepared and provided to us by a local parish. They'd make a single batch of peanut butter sandwiches to last us the entire week and then deliver them to us all at once. We'd store the weekly batch of sandwiches in our refrigerator to keep them as fresh as possible.

As you can probably guess, by the end of the week the sandwiches were not great, as the bread had hardened. I didn't want to hand out week-old sandwiches, but there wasn't budget in place to purchase food for distribution. The way things were when I took over, which was how things were run by my predecessor, was that we were supposed to work with what was available to us through donations. We weren't supposed to spend money. That was the golden rule. Don't spend money. What? Why not? What's the good in having money coming in if we weren't spending it on things that actually went to helping the people we were serving?

While I understood why the system was the way it was, I knew I wanted to change it. Updating our morning food distribution options was one of my first steps into making sure we were meeting the needs of the homeless community with dignity. If I wasn't willing to eat a week-old sandwich, I wasn't willing to serve it. If there wasn't the budget for it, I'd make sure we raised the money to create a budget for it. Soon enough, we had new solutions in place, one of which being we started preparing sandwiches in-house every day.

One of the changes I added into our morning menu right away was offering cups of water. How could you eat a peanut butter sandwich without something to drink? This didn't make sense to me. But there wasn't money in the budget at the time to buy cups to provide water. This was long before individual bottles of water were a thing. I soon figured out a way for us to get cups donated. Problem solved.

As money was raised and donations increased, we were able to expand what we served daily. One of our first upgrades was serving coffee. We had received a couple of big stainless steel coffee urns and could prepare enough coffee each day to provide everyone with a warm cup of it, which was a luxury item on cold mornings.

I remember at one point we had a bunch of hot dogs donated to us. To be able to serve them we needed to cook them. We used what we had available to us. Since those coffee urns boiled water, we cleaned one out, filled it with water for boiling and stuffed it with hot dogs. The coffee urn-cooked hot dogs were a hit. Everyone was thrilled to be receiving meat for breakfast.

Soon enough we added bologna sandwiches. Bologna worked well because it is an inexpensive cold cut. Plus, I love bologna sandwiches! I ate them as a boy and I eat them still. My nephew Patrick, who lives with me right now, can't believe I like to eat bologna sandwiches on white bread with nothing else on it—no condiments, nothing. Bread and meat, that's it. Some things we have in our childhood stick with us and when I was a kid bologna sandwiches were a luxury for us. By adding bologna sandwiches into our morning handout rotation at St. Vincent de Paul, we were providing protein consistently, which was a step up.

Since we were making sandwiches fresh every day, we had additional food distribution-related needs, which meant we had more people volunteering to help. I remember Judy Benson, who's been a generous donor over the years, used to come down and help us cut bologna and prepare those sandwiches. Every once in a while, when we visit, Judy and I reflect on those early years that included making sandwiches in the thrift store.

Recently, I've found myself thinking back to those early days of our work more and more. Over the years, a lot has been built and developed, and we've helped many individuals and families. From the time I was assigned to St. Vincent de Paul in 1982 until I retired in 2011, we served millions of hot meals to our neighbors in need. But momentum for what all that would become, including our ability to provide millions of meals, grew from serving peanut butter sandwiches out the side door of a warehouse thrift store.

50.

The Travelator

By the end of the first year in my new job, I was spending a lot of time raising money so we could build the multimillion-dollar St. Vincent de Paul Center. We needed money first and foremost because without it, we couldn't build. Fundraising was my main focus. But soon enough I realized I didn't know enough about what it meant to actually shelter people. I'd never run a shelter. I'd never spent much time within a shelter other than touring other facilities. I was working with a drafted design concept for the building I thought could solve the problem. But what did I really know?

Everyone had been telling me what the problem was and many people had suggestions for how to solve it. But I figured, if I'm building the building and I'm responsible for it, I want to know and experience firsthand what the problem is.

I met with Bishop Maher and told him my concerns. I

admitted I didn't know what I didn't know, and I needed to learn more. I asked him to let me start sheltering people in a leased building. I needed to experience it to know what I was doing. He agreed.

Soon enough, we found a space to rent in downtown. Well before the St. Vincent de Paul Center was built, which took about five years from idea to opening, our first shelter was in the Travelator Motor Hotel. It was in north downtown San Diego across the street from the El Cortez Hotel, which was a classy hotel at the time where a lot of events were held: weddings, high school proms, holiday parties, galas. The Travelator was a lower-end motel-style place that had previously been used as a homeless shelter run by another agency. The interior of the building hadn't been well cared for and we were able to lease it for a reasonable price.

We started serving meals and sheltering people right away. But we didn't have much in the way of a kitchen to use other than a standard-size four-burner stove and oven in what had been the manager's apartment within the Travelator. Sister Fay Hagen was working with me by then and she came up with the idea of using catering warmers to keep food hot and ready to serve. She'd cook a pot of spaghetti and put it in a warmer. Then she'd cook another pot of spaghetti and put it in another warmer. She had a rotation system with a few pots and a few warmers going all at once so we'd always have enough hot food ready to serve.

We were creating solutions as we went. We just dove in and

did what was needed to get it done. I've always focused on creating solutions and I'm fortunate to have always had people around me who did the same. I give a lot of credit to nuns. Nuns in the old days, when they didn't have anything, they made do. I was educated by nuns in Catholic school; I knew to listen to them. Nuns are hard workers. They are tireless. Sister Fay was like that, and she'd start things without telling me. She did what was needed when it was needed, always to support the greater good of our mission of helping and serving the needs of others. And when she'd come to me with a new idea, I'd say, "do it." I trusted her. I never held anyone back from taking initiative.

Also around the same time of us opening the Travelator, we had rented a warehouse at 8th and J streets where we provided daily meals for unsheltered San Diegans. We had grown to serving well over 200 people every morning from the St. Vincent de Paul Thrift Store and needed a better facility to provide meals, including an area where our unsheltered neighbors could sit down to eat their meals. We partnered with an organization called Catholic Worker and moved our meal distribution over to the newly rented warehouse. It didn't have a kitchen, so we had prepared food brought in to provide everyone in need with quality hot meals every day. Eventually, that program grew to be so big that we took it over ourselves and Catholic Worker continued doing service work in other ways as it had been for many years.

The Travelator had one big meeting-style room we used

throughout the day for different things. In the morning, it was where we served breakfast. When breakfast was done, it was used for school. Then it was used for lunch. In the afternoon, it was used as a medical clinic or whatever else we had going on. Then in the evening, we served dinner in there.

One day I got a call from a woman named Mary Case. She had been working at a Salvation Army shelter that was closing down and heard about what we were doing. She asked to meet with me. Mary and I went out to lunch and she basically told me I needed to hire her. Which I did. Hiring Mary was a great decision. She was responsible for running all our programs for years, and she started her work with us from the Travelator. She'd often just tell me how we were going to be doing something and I'd agree to everything she said. If she said we needed more staff, we hired more staff. If she said we needed money for this or that, I figured out how to raise the money we needed so we could do what she suggested. I trusted her.

I've always put a lot of trust in my staff. I trusted they knew what they were doing and if they didn't, they figured it out. I stayed out of their way, and they stayed out of mine. In time, it was clear what our roles were. I raised money and they ran programs. It worked.

51.

Education is Empowerment

While I mainly stayed out of the day-to-day operations of what the staff was doing to develop and run our programs, I was clear about wanting our overall approach to be educational. My degree is in education, so I saw everything we did as some form of education. I understood early on that I wanted what we were doing to be more than meals and beds. I was always aware enough to know that people had to be educated to be able to get out of their troubles. So, from the time we started sheltering people at the Travelator and creating programs, everything we did was from an educational approach. You have to teach people how to get out of poverty.

At the time when we started, approximately 40 percent of people experiencing homelessness were illiterate. That meant they couldn't read a job application—and if you can't get past the application, you can't get the job.

In the days when I was young, you'd go to a warehouse and

say, "I want a job," and if you could lift boxes, they'd hire you. Can you drive a car? If you said yes, they gave you the keys. They didn't ask to see your license. No forms. No applications. You didn't worry about all that stuff. It was a different world. Well, those days are long gone.

I knew if we were really going to help people try to get out of homelessness we had to concentrate on some form of education being our foundation. We started with the basics. We taught reading and writing. To help people get off drugs, we had to teach about drugs and addiction. We had experts come in to help us with counseling and educating. We had a lot of latitude to just help our neighbors with what they needed directly.

We could do all of this at that time because there weren't all these rules that exist now. Homelessness wasn't an issue for everybody then—people weren't talking about it much. We could address the problem without people telling us what we could or couldn't do.

When we were starting out, there wasn't an easy way to get information about homelessness. We didn't have computers with tons of data to access like there is now. We didn't have the internet. So, I started asking a lot of questions. I started talking to people about homelessness, and not just people who ran shelters or had experience serving the poor and homeless. I asked people who were living on the streets— the people we were sheltering at the Travelator. I wanted to understand their stories so we could understand what was needed. My staff did the same.

Something I found out right away was there were more than just men who were homeless. This was news to me. This was back in the early 1980s, and my understanding at that time was it was only single men, mostly drunken bums, who were homeless. I didn't know much and that was my perception because that is what I could see. I soon learned that was not the case at all. I came to understand that women and children were homeless, too. But they just weren't as visible as men. Women with children tended to lay low during the day and that's why I'd usually only see men wandering the streets. When I discovered this, our plans had to be adjusted. I immediately realized I no longer was designing a shelter for single men; I needed to house women and children as well.

This meant our programs were designed to accommodate children, women, and men. It became a whole other level of sheltering our neighbors and developing programs to empower all people we were serving, especially kids. I knew if these kids were going to live a life of homelessness in the system as it was, they were most likely going to become homeless adults, too, and their kids were going to become homeless. Without programs in place to help educate them and empower them with opportunities to grow themselves and develop self-worth, we would perpetuate the cycle—and I didn't want to do that.

I wanted us to help stop the cycle of homelessness and poverty as much as we could. Education was the logical approach forward to help. We started out informally educating kids in our shelter. Then, through Sister Fay's insistence, we were successful in forming the first school for homeless children within a shelter.

Sister Fay had written a few letters to the superintendent of the San Diego Unified School District about the unique needs of the kids in our shelter and the superintendent paid attention. The superintendent was nearing retirement and he really took to the idea. Before he retired, he made sure our school was approved to be a legitimate city school.

This was a whole new concept that had never been done before, but it met the needs of the families, because otherwise many of the parents would lose their children to the system. At the time in the mid-1980s, if a child was out of school for a period of three months—I don't remember the exact time frame rules but let's just say three months— that was considered child abuse and the state could take your child away from you.

So, let's say you're homeless and your child hasn't been going to school for a while. Then you get into a shelter and your child who hasn't attended school for a few months goes back; that school was legally responsible to report the neglect of education to the county. Then because of neglect, the county would have cause to come and take your child away. Homeless parents knew all this, so they'd just keep their children out of school. They didn't want to lose them.

That meant those children wouldn't learn the basics, much

less anything else; there'd be a whole generation growing up without even a grade school education. And without an education, the cycle of homelessness will repeat.

But if they lived in our shelter and went to our school, an actual accredited school, when they subsequently went to another school, they'd be transferring from one school to another and no one asked questions. So that's what we did. We created the first school within a homeless shelter.

52.

Model for Change

When I was a parish priest and someone came to the door needing shelter, our solution was to send them over to the Salvation Army or Catholic Charities. They handled it all. I wasn't in the mix of serving people in need that way. Yet as I started my job at St. Vincent de Paul and became more aware of how other agencies worked within the current model, I could see what was working and what wasn't. It was apparent to me that people were cycling through the system, never getting off the streets. I didn't want to perpetuate a miserable life for them. I knew I had to come up with something new if we were going to create different results— results that could help people by stopping the cycle.

I didn't want to turn anyone away, and what we were faced with was seeing single men, single women, and families all needing housing. I wanted to house them all—all together under one roof. Well, this wasn't being done. Many people told me it couldn't work. They said you can't have men and women in the same shelter. But that didn't make any sense to me because when they moved out they'd be living in a mixed environment everywhere else. I felt they had to learn how to live in a mixed environment and there was no better place to do that than with us. That's what we did from day one at the Travelator and it carried through. Of course, we've always been smart and safe with security in place and that increased to cameras and everything we needed to ensure people were cared for and protected.

I'm a great believer that it's how you manage people through experiencing homelessness that makes the difference. Just like it's how you manage diabetes or how you manage caring for someone who has cancer. You can't cure it, but you can help manage them through it so they can live longer and live better. We basically had to learn how to manage the fact that we were going to have a mixed population living within our community, just as they'd experience after they left. We provided a place of transition, something that wasn't being done in other shelters.

And we did more things that were different than the traditional homeless shelter "three hots and a cot" approach. In that sheltering model, people could normally only stay seven days maximum.

I rejected that model. I knew our neighbors needed to stay longer. I knew they needed more time. Why? Because people need time to change. If a person's lived a certain lifestyle for ten or twenty years, it can't change in seven days. It just can't. None of us can do that. We need time to adjust patterns. I wanted us to be able to house people for longer.

Considering I didn't have any hands-on experience with any other model, I couldn't take no for an answer. For example, one time I asked the folks at the Salvation Army shelter, "Why don't you keep people during the day?" They were the experts. They had been doing it longer. It made sense to ask them. They responded, "It costs more money to keep people during the day."

So, the only reason someone wasn't getting services during the day was money? Really? There was a simple solution to this. Raise more money.

It seemed to me that money was actually being wasted by putting people up only for the night and then kicking them out for the entire day. Any good that may have been done within their shelter just walked out the door into the circumstance that contributed to them being sheltered in the first place. That didn't make logical sense to me.

I didn't want to waste money, and I didn't want money to be the reason we weren't taking care of the real needs of our neighbors. If we were going to have any hope of stopping the cycle, we needed to do something different. The more I learned, the more it made the most sense to keep people twenty-four hours a day. No shelter in America at that time, that I know of, was doing that. But no matter what everyone else was doing and had been doing for years, it didn't make any sense to me to put people back out on the street all day. So we didn't. We created a new model of community for people experiencing homelessness. Some thought this was a revolutionary concept. To me, it was just common sense.

As we learned about what people truly needed, programs were created to help them have the chance to empower themselves to change. Extending past the seven-day cap and welcoming in twenty-four-hour care, we started housing neighbors in need for longer and longer. And years later, we developed a program that empowered people to be able to stay with us for up to two years as they gained education and job training.

53.

Neighbors in Need

While many people think they have the solution to homelessness, the truth is homelessness has always existed. Story after story in the Bible shares about people without homes. This is why I don't think it will ever be non-existent. Jesus spoke of it. I trust Jesus.

So, to me, it's not been about creating the solution that will end homelessness for good for everyone. My approach has always been for us to do whatever we could to help as many people as possible have access to housing and opportunities to help improve their lives.

Jesus spoke often about giving to the poor and helping those in need. Jesus instructed everyone to "love thy neighbor as thyself" and that's what I was to do. Treat my neighbors in need as I'd treat myself. I want nice housing for myself. I'd only lived in rectories and seminaries, and we live well. Our places are nice. I wanted to create nice housing for our neighbors in need.

Nice to me for the St. Vincent de Paul building meant bedrooms with beds not cots, a playground for children, and fountains in the courtyard. I wanted someone to walk in and feel like they were at a nice motel. I didn't want what we were building to be another standard shelter. For children, especially, I wanted it to be a place they wanted to be.

Let's say a child walks into another shelter that isn't nice inside. "We have to stay here?"

But then, a child walks into our place and sees a courtyard with a playground and fountains. "Wow, do we get to stay here?" There's excitement. It's a whole different attitude toward the experience. Mom and Dad suddenly aren't failures; now they're successes. Yes, they are still in a shelter, but as far as the children are concerned, it's, "Look what I have now. I have this nice place to stay." I wanted children to feel good about being with us, even if it was just for a short while. I wanted adults to feel good, too.

Feeling good from the moment someone walks in the door is the start of an attitude change. Men and women living on the street for whatever reason and for whatever length of time typically aren't feeling so good about themselves. Their attitudes about themselves and their circumstances are negative. I wanted to help people change their attitudes about themselves. I wanted to help them have dignity— knowing they matter and are worthy of respect. I wanted our model to be a compassionate approach to helping meet the needs of our neighbors with empathy and respect. No one is trash to be cast aside like they don't matter. God doesn't make junk. Everyone is a child of God and deserves to be treated as such. Everyone is our neighbor. Everyone!

Our programs were designed to empower our neighbors in need to improve their lives over a period of time. The ultimate goal is graduating out of St. Vincent de Paul to be self-sufficient and break the cycle of poverty they found themselves in. For me, it was essential that we treated everyone who walked through our door with dignity and respect from the moment they arrived. Compassion is the doorway to change. Everything else follows from there.

In the years to come, we developed what is known now as Father Joe's Villages CREED. Everyone on staff is dedicated to providing our neighbors in need with compassion, respect, empathy, empowerment, and dignity.

54.

Home Run Hustler

Long before we had broken ground to have a place with a playground and fountains, I was struggling to raise money. In fact, my first two years on the job were brutal for fundraising. Everyone said "no" to me. We did have individual contributors making monthly donations, which helped tremendously—and some of these people have been donating monthly for all these years, even still. But I needed to raise millions of dollars, and I just wasn't getting anywhere with seeking out major donors from grants, foundations, or corporate sponsors. I was just another person running another charity trying to get money. I wasn't well known, and I didn't have any influence. The project needed sizable funding support and I had no experience seeking out large-scale donations. Every letter I sent out to solicit foundation grant money received a "no" response or no reply at all.

I was doing my best to tell the story of what we were doing and why it was important and needed, but we just weren't getting much visibility at the time.

But then, we hit our first big break in the fall of 1984.

Clayton Brace was the general manager of Channel 10 at the time and he decided to adopt me as his focused charity. He knew what I was trying to do to get a funding campaign going and he wanted to help get the word out. He decided to donate the production of a professionally produced commercial and free air time on Channel 10 for it to run. He didn't want his in-house staff to film the commercial. Instead, he wanted to hire a man he knew to write and produce it who had received all kinds of awards for television and film production. They got it all organized, and I went in to shoot the commercial.

When I showed up, they handed me the script of what I was supposed to say into the camera. The first line read, "Hi. I'm Father Joe. I'm a hustler. I'm here to hustle you out of your money."

As I read it, I was shocked. I said, "I can't say that! I'm a priest. Are you kidding me?"

But the producer insisted it was the right script to use. I pushed back a bit. He countered, "Look, you either trust me on this or you guys need to find someone else."

As I read more of the script, I saw in the next part I'd share about how we were helping neighbors in need and how viewers could help. It was simple and did include the important information that needed to be shared. I trusted that he knew what he was doing. This was his profession. I decided to do it.

My first television commercial for St. Vincent de Paul aired on October 6, 1984. I know the date because it was a really important day for the city of San Diego; it was the day of game four of the National League Championship between the San Diego Padres and Chicago Cubs. This was the first time for the Padres to make it that far and everyone in town was either at the game or watching it on television—on Channel 10.

At the time, the National League Championship was a best-of-five series. The Cubs won the first two games. The Padres won the third game. Game four was critical because if the Padres lost, the Cubs would go to the World Series. But if the Padres won game four, the series would be tied up and progress to a series finale game five to determine which team would move on.

Game four was exciting down to the last inning. At the bottom of the ninth, the score was tied 5–5. When Steve Garvey got up to bat, he hit a two-run home run to win the game. Everyone went nuts! It was a huge moment. Then, when Channel 10 cut to commercial immediately following that game-winning homer, there I was looking at everyone through their television screen saying, "Hi. I'm Father Joe. I'm a hustler."

I couldn't have dreamed up a more perfect moment for the commercial to air. Everyone saw it! From that moment on,

I became known as the hustler priest. I'd run into people on the street and they'd say, "Aren't you that hustler priest who's on TV?" It worked and we kept using it.

Whenever I was on television or being written about, I was the hustler priest. It made me stand out. It caught people's attention. "What did they just say about that priest?" Then, with their attention captured, people paid closer attention to what I was saying, which drew more attention to what we were doing, and that was the whole point. The commercial was a home run for us. The Padres went on to win game five and be the 1984 National League Champions. Even though they didn't end up winning the World Series, that season was historic. A spotlight was shining on San Diego baseball and just our luck, on St. Vincent de Paul, too.

55.

Copley Surprise

That commercial provided the visibility we needed. Channel 10 continued to run it, and I became more recognizable to people in San Diego. I just kept popping up on everyone's television throughout the day and night. I got calls for interviews with other news stations and the local newspaper. The more interviews I had, the more opportunities for interviews I was offered.

My visibility created the publicity we needed. I was developing a media presence with the local news to be able to talk about what we were doing and why it mattered to San Diegans. I was forming relationships with media producers who decided what stories were being run, and of course was always pitching stories to them about what we were doing. It was the start of what would become an ongoing media presence in San Diego for me, all of which was about making sure the work we were doing at St. Vincent de Paul got exposure and remained relevant.

Our mailbox started filling up with donation envelopes with checks in them. We have always done a lot of mailings. In those early years, especially, mailings were the main way we sought out donations. Every letter we sent out included a St. Vincent de Paul return-addressed envelope for a potential donor to send a donation check back to us. Whenever we saw those envelopes in our mail, we knew money was inside.

My mail came to me, including all the foundation grant decline letters. I had sent out over a hundred letters to all the big foundations and I was used to opening envelopes containing letters on their professional letterhead saying, "Thank you for your inquiry but…" I was used to being declined.

One day, as I was sitting at my desk opening up "no" letter after "no" letter, I opened up a letter that said, "We are pleased to…" What's this? Wait a minute. This is a "yes" and there's a check. I turned over the check to see the amount and practically fell out of my chair. The Copley Foundation had sent in a donation check for $250,000! I could barely believe what I was seeing. I shot up from my desk chair to show the check to everyone on staff.

The Copley Foundation donation was a major breakthrough for us. It provided validation for our building project. To have the Copley Foundation behind us as our first major donor gave us clout. It meant they believed in what we were doing and if they were on board, others would be more willing to be on board, too. Naturally, I made sure we got news coverage about their donation and how it would advance the project forward. Soon, we announced plans to break ground on St. Vincent de Paul Center.

56.

Breaking Ground

With local publicity increasing and having secured our first major donor, everything started developing at a faster pace. Word started getting out well beyond San Diego, which was apparent when I got call from the producers at 60 Minutes. They wanted to do a story on us and this new idea I had on homelessness. Since 60 Minutes didn't do fluff pieces and was known for its investigative reporting, we all wondered, "What did we do wrong? Why would 60 Minutes want to investigate us?"

They let us know they wanted to do a feature story on us because of the idea of building a new type of shelter. The idea of building a beautiful building and offering a whole new approach to homelessness was foreign to them. No one else was doing this and they wanted to come out to San Diego and cover it.

Harry Reasoner did the story. He interviewed some of our early donors, plus Judge Robert C. Coates and a couple city politicians. They all went on the streets and lived among the people to experience homelessness firsthand—to see how others were treated. They got the normal treatment, with people ignoring them and treating them like dirt. It was amazing because they had no clue how it really was until they experienced it.

I didn't partake in this experiment. At some point, Harry Reasoner asked me why I didn't do it with them. I told him I didn't need to find out what homelessness is all about. I work with the homeless every day; I already know what they need. That's my job.

The folks at 60 Minutes toured the Travelator to see what we were doing and how our programs were helping men, women, and children. They were there for the 1985 groundbreaking ceremony for what would become St. Vincent de Paul Joan Kroc Center. When the show aired on national television, it gave us a new level of exposure. People from all over the country were paying attention. We were in the spotlight, but also a spotlight was on me to actually do what I said I was going to do.

57.

Joan's Jet

One day I was in my office and got a call from Joan Kroc's secretary. She told me Joan was headed downtown and wanted to stop in and talk with me. When Joan arrived, she walked into the thrift store dressed in casual clothing. Everyone who was working wanted to meet her. She was friendly, greeting everyone as they exchanged hellos. The staff was beside themselves.

Joan, who owned the Padres at the time, told me she had watched my commercials on television, and wanted to meet me and hear more about my plans. We talked for a little while about everything. I shared about the project, what stage in the process we were with constructing the new building, and our projection for completion. Soon, she told me she had to get going because her new jet was arriving at the airport and she needed to be there when it came in. As she stood up, she let me know that she'd be donating a half million dollars. I was stunned and immediately made a joke, "Is that for me or the project?" We both laughed.

I asked her if she'd like me to bless her new plane. She welcomed that idea. Joan suggested, "How about you get the holy water and meet me there. We'll go right now."

That's how it started—a spontaneous meeting, a blessed plane, and a check for $500,000.

That was Joan's way. She was gracious and generous. She told me once about how she'd pay attention to the news about what was going on in the city, where there were needs. She'd read the newspaper every day and cut out articles about charities and the projects they were working on. Then, usually at the end of the year, she'd write checks to all the charities she wanted to help—typically doing it as a surprise. Surprise, a check from Joan Kroc just arrived. She was something else.

58.

Getting Fired

What I originally guessed would be a $3.5 million project became a $7 million building once it was in motion and construction bids were in place. It was 1986. I was about four years into my job, and we had broken ground the year prior. We had raised enough money by then to meet the $7 million budget. But there was a big issue. The project was $4 million over budget. It was going to cost $11 million to complete.

Bishop Maher was furious with me for spending so much money. He said we needed to stop construction right away. But at that time, we had only built one floor and framed the second. It wouldn't look right. Plus, the basement parking level was underway, which was one of the main reasons we were over budget. We didn't have the parking garage as part of the original plans or budget. But once construction was going, it came to my attention that we would need our own parking. At the time, some people disagreed with me because the east side of downtown San Diego wasn't busy—parking wasn't an issue. But I disagreed. We dug out the garage after the first level was already in place. That was expensive. But now, decades later, downtown is developed so much that we don't have nearly enough parking even with that garage.

Bishop Maher finally agreed to carry on with construction. Since the project was within a year of its projected finishing date, time was running short. We had no other choice than to come up with the money to complete construction. Bishop Maher decided he'd loan me the $4 million that was needed and not one penny more. Yet, I was responsible for raising the money to pay him back.

Even so, Bishop Maher was not happy with me at all. He decided to relieve me of all decision-making duties by appointing another priest to be the new administrator for St. Vincent de Paul. He was basically firing me from all responsibilities except for being the media guy who raised money. He put someone else in my place just like that.

Then, a few days later, Joan Kroc calls me on the phone. I had only met her once in person and we'd never talked on the phone before. She told me she was calling to see how the project was going. I gave her an update, and then told her we were $4 million short. Joan told me not to worry. She'd send me $3 million tomorrow. What? I was stunned. Soon enough, we hung up and I thought to myself, "Did that just happen?"

Later that evening, I got a call from her lawyer saying, "Joan wasn't sure you believed it was really her." Which was sort of true. The timing of it all was hard to believe. I had been fired over money a few days earlier, and then Joan calls me out of the blue and says she's going to send me most of the money I needed to finish. Surprise!

My mind was swift to think of asking for one favor. I said, "When you send me the check, can you write a note that says only Father Joe can spend the money?"

Next thing you know, a $3 million check signed by Joan Kroc shows up with a letter stating that only Father Joe was allowed to spend the money. And just like that, I had my full job back. The other priest was appointed to work at Catholic Charities instead and I was back to running things.

St. Vincent de Paul Joan Kroc Center opened in 1987.

59.

One-Stop Shop

Upon opening, we were able to immediately provide housing solutions for 315 neighbors in need. In addition to serving three meals a day for residents in our program, we continued serving unsheltered neighbors in need with a daily hot meal just as we had been doing for a few years prior from the other buildings we rented. We simply moved over to our new building. It was designed purposefully with a fantastic full-service industrial kitchen that was more than suitable for handling everything needed for preparing and serving thousands of hot meals every day.

Our building design included a sizable dining area for residents to eat together. We also included a dining area for unsheltered San Diegans to sit down for their meals as well. From day one of opening that first newly built building, we've been focused on meeting the needs of our neighbors in need with care and compassion, whether they are living within our housing programs or living on the streets. During the summer months, it can get really hot for unsheltered neighbors who are standing in line awaiting meals. To make things comfortable, we got huge wall-sized air-conditioning fans set up in the courtyard to provide cooling comfort as they waited. I have always come from the frame of mind that if I'd want it for me, I'd provide it for them and if I wouldn't want it for me, I'd never consider it for them. Jesus's words are always ringing in my mind to love my neighbor as myself, treat my neighbor as myself. Since I like nice housing, hot delicious meals, and being comfortable, that was the standard for everything we provided for our neighbors in need.

Another thing I like is one-stop-shopping. Perhaps it's the Bronx kid in me where everything we ever needed was basically on our block or within a block of us. But ever since I moved to California, I have enjoyed going to one shopping center to get everything I need. For years, my favorite place to shop in downtown San Diego was Horton Plaza, because everything I needed was there. I didn't have to go all over town to get things from a bunch of different stores. That's a waste of time to me. Everything I needed was in one location. Horton Plaza opened in 1985, right around the same time we were breaking ground. While I didn't model anything after it, we were both builders in downtown essentially offering a similar solution: a one-stop-shop. Horton Plaza had everything you'd need within one property and so did we.

Also at that time, many of my board members were executives for major hotels and this one-stop-shop was what hotels were moving their business model to as well. When you go to a hotel, it's not just rooms within the property. Many hotels now have one or two restaurants, shops, a business center, a beauty salon, and even a spa. Why do they do this? They don't want you leaving. They want you to do everything you need within their property. This is the same with cruise ships. I love taking cruises! You can pretty much do anything and everything on the ship that you can do on land. Hotels, cruise ships, and shopping centers offered one-stop-shop solutions and so did we. It just made sense.

I wanted people in our program to remain with us. I wanted us to handle all their needs. It didn't make any sense to me to house people overnight and then send them to other places to get what they needed. I felt by doing that we'd lose momentum for progress. We'd lose control. By having everything under one roof, we would be able to help facilitate rehabilitation opportunities more effectively.

Besides, if I was sending people to someone else's program for assistance and that program lost its funding and went out of business, what then? I didn't want anyone else having that much influence over our progress. We needed to keep it all in-house if we were going to really be able to help our neighbors get off the streets for good, which was and always has been the ultimate goal.

If you wonder how we got so far over budget on our first build, it was also because of this one-stop-shop solution. We didn't just construct a building to provide beds. We built a center for creating opportunities to help build up people! By offering a one-stop-shop, we could provide rehabilitation opportunities for our neighbors experiencing homelessness with the purpose of meeting them where they were at and giving them the time and resources they needed to create real changes in their lives.

Within our onsite programs we offered a full-service medical clinic; onsite public accredited school for youth, GED preparation, and adult education classes; job training center; mental health support, peer groups, and addiction treatment and support; full-service kitchen and dining to feed thousands of people daily; and necessities for clothing and personal hygiene for people of all ages. Everything someone needed was available because we provided a one-stop-shop.

This was a whole new model for creating solutions for homelessness. To me, this one-stop-shop concept focused on providing a complete restart to someone's life. We were focused on a whole-person approach to tackle all of the issues that perpetuated the cycle of homelessness and poverty. To help our neighbors have the chance to change their lives, we needed to meet them where they were at and help them have access to everything they needed to create a fresh start forward for themselves. We became builders of buildings to be able to help build up our community of neighbors in need. We weren't trying to be revolutionary. It was just common sense to me.

Our first building ran way over budget for all the right

reasons. Our one-stop-shop solution had everything our neighbors in need needed. But what I will never live down is that underground garage. Who starts digging out an underground parking garage after construction had started? You already know the answer: a priest who had no experience doing what he was doing, but was willing to learn and adjust plans as he went along. While it was the big-ticket item that shot us over budget, everyone is glad we have it now because parking in downtown is scarce.

60.

Pardon Me, Do You Have Any Grey Poupon?

Sometime within that first year of opening St. Vincent de Paul Joan Kroc Center, I was reading in a magazine about a foundation in London that offered an award for unique housing developments. Each year through its World Habitat Awards program, the foundation recognized the most outstanding innovative housing solutions in the world. The grand prize was $16,000 and of course significant recognition.

This sounded great to me and we applied. I thought we were a perfect fit since St. Vincent de Paul Joan Kroc Center was an innovative housing solution for people experiencing homelessness through the unique concept of providing everything under one roof, which was a brand new idea at that time. Something else unique about us was that our newly constructed building was built specifically for people experiencing homelessness and only with their needs in mind. No one else was actually building new beautiful buildings for homeless people. Normally, what was used for sheltering people was some sort of old, rundown warehouse-type building. Along with new and nice accommodations, we were offering amenities and programs to help rehabilitate and empower our neighbors in need. No one else was doing any of this at the time that I knew of, not in our country or anywhere else in the world.

The foundation reviewed our application and its team came over from London to study us and see what we were doing. For one thing, they were shocked that we actually had homeless people. The perception of the US was that we were the richest country in the world at the time—the land of opportunity. How is it that we could have homelessness?

Beyond that, they wanted to see if it actually worked. They wanted to see for themselves if we were actually offering a nice, dignified housing solution for people experiencing homelessness, plus opportunities for rehabilitation to improve their lives. Did we really have schooling and job training, and provide medical care all under one roof, and did it actually work? They had never seen anything like it before and yes, we were in fact doing all those things.

The World Habitat Awards committee did select us as the winner that year.

When you win an award, you have to go get it. The recognition ceremony was in London—and we made a big deal of it. We put together a group discount rate for airfare and hotel and offered it to whoever wanted to go. While everyone had to pay their own way, we did cover some of the expenses for some staff members. We ended up having a good-size group go to London to attend the awards ceremony: some staff and board members, some women from the Ladies Guild, and Joan Kroc.

Joan was flying to London on her jet and invited me to accompany her. I said yes. That was my first time on a private jet. The only other time I had been near Joan's jet was when I blessed it that day she dropped by to visit me in my warehouse thrift store office. Fast forward a few years to us flying to London on that same jet to get an award for a building she helped us build; it was just unreal.

Needless to say, a few interesting things happened on that trip to London. For starters, the flight attendant woke us up in the morning to let us know we were making a stop in Newfoundland because Joan wanted to have fresh lobster for breakfast. What? We are stopping to get lobster for breakfast? Wow, okay. This was a whole different experience for me—a priest who lived in a parish rectory finding himself jetting to the United Kingdom on a private airplane making a quick stop for lobster.

It was like living in a fantasy world for a brief amount of time, which was apparent on the flight back after the award ceremony. Since Joan was flying on to Paris, I went back to normal life, flying home coach class on British Airways with everyone else.

When we arrived at the airport in London after our lobster

stop, the customs and immigration people came out to meet us at Joan's jet. We didn't stand in a line to get approved for entry. No, they came to us. I had never experienced that before. Then we got into two different Jaguar limousines. Yes, Jaguar limousines. I had no idea Jaguar actually made limousines. Since we were staying at two different hotels, Joan at some luxury hotel and me with the rest of the group at our more basic hotel, our limousines drove away in two different directions.

A few minutes into the ride, the phone inside of my limousine rang. Remember, this was before everyone had mobile phones and having a car phone at that time was a luxury item; not many people had them. I had not talked on a car phone before. The driver answered the call and then said, "Excuse me, Father Joe Carroll, there's a call for you."

What? I couldn't imagine who knew where I was to call me on a car phone driving through London in a limousine. I took the receiver and said, "Hello?"

On the other end of the line, I heard Joan say, "Pardon me, do you have any Grey Poupon?"

For those of you too young to remember, a popular commercial many years ago featured a man eating in a limo, when a second limo pulls beside and its passenger asks him that question. Joan and I laughed. For a kid from the Bronx, this was a whole new experience for me and Joan made it especially enjoyable.

Soon enough, I met up with the rest of the group. There were about thirty of us there from San Diego. At the World Habitat Awards ceremony, the Archbishop of Canterbury presented the award to me and Jim Mulvaney Sr., who was the chairman of our board of directors at the time. It was a really special event.

Receiving that award was a symbol of all the purposeful work many people had done to get us to that point. The award was for all of us to share together—the countless donors, volunteers, staff, and board members. Everyone helped make it happen.

All the work everyone had done to get us to that point—donors, volunteers, staff, board members—meant the award was for all of us. From starting by serving peanut butter sandwiches from the side of a warehouse thrift store and learning about what was really needed to create solutions by renting a motel to use as a shelter to building a multimillion-dollar housing solution for neighbors experiencing homelessness, everyone helped make it happen.

I recall months after that trip, while talking with someone about it, the award, and the check for $16,000, I said, "Never was so much money spent for so small of a check."

61.

Josue House

In the late 1980s, AIDS was becoming more prevalent. People were getting sick and dying. There weren't any drug treatments like there are now. At the time, there wasn't very much information about it at all other than if you got it, you died. No one knew how it was being transmitted. People were scared of catching it. It was a terrible disease and was taking the lives of men, women, and children.

It was common for people who became infected with AIDS to lose their job, which meant they couldn't pay their bills and they'd become homeless. They had nowhere to go. Because of the stigma around the disease and everyone's fear of catching it, many people were denied care, compassion, and dignity by their own families. They needed somewhere to go. We opened the first Josue House in 1988 to help provide hospice for people dying of AIDS.

It was Sister Fay who first brought this idea to me. She had a priest friend who was dying of AIDS. As his illness progressed, she wanted to help. Sister Fay went to San Francisco to learn more about AIDS and find out how people were being cared for there. She was there for a few months, learning about the disease and how to care for those who had it. When she returned, she wanted us to do something for people with AIDS in our city.

It wasn't going unnoticed that the Catholic church in San Diego wasn't doing anything yet to help people with AIDS. The gay community was protesting the church and the Bishop. They weren't happy with us. But the truth is, for a while we just didn't know enough about AIDS to know what we needed to do about it. While Bishop Maher ended up getting a lot of credit when we did start housing and caring for people with AIDS, it's Sister Fay who deserves all the credit for getting the wheels in motion for it.

Sister Fay came to me with the idea of us having a specific home just for people with AIDS, so they could be cared for with compassion and dignity. At the time, we owned a house on 70th Street that was vacant. It had been donated to us from Robert Hartson, the founder of Hartson Ambulance Service. We decided that would be the right place to use, and I went to Bishop Maher to get approval, which he granted.

The four-bedroom house had been used for Hartson's ambulance business and wasn't readily in shape for residents. But next thing you know, the Ladies Guild had that house all spruced up—cleaned top to bottom and beautifully decorated. It was a really nice place!

Sister Fay developed a relationship with the medical clinic at UCSD, so whenever a patient came in who needed care and had nowhere to go, they'd call us. We were able to house ten to twelve patients at a time. It was a difficult time for them, as they basically came to us to die. When they left to go to the hospital, they didn't come back.

Our staff did everything possible to create a peaceful home, especially since many of the men and women had been completely rejected by their families. I had to get involved a few times, pleading with parents to visit their son or daughter before they died. Some parents just plain refused; they were shutting out and denying their children for having the disease and rejecting them for being gay. It was an emotional trip.

I would plead with parents and ultimately the only thing I could say in the end was, "Your child is going to die. It's not that they may die or they could die. They are going to die. Do you really want their last thing to be your rejection?" Some came and many didn't. It was heartbreaking.

When AIDS first hit and no one knew how it was being spread, people thought you could get it by shaking hands or hugging. That meant many people who had AIDS were often refused basic human touch from anyone, especially their family and friends. Our staff knew better, so holding their hands was part of our care regimen. Also, for many of our residents, their partners weren't allowed to visit with them when they were in hospital-provided hospice care since they weren't legally recognized spouses for medical consent. At our place, they could visit and spend time together.

We kept the home private as much as we could, but soon enough we had an issue with the neighbor next door. There was a man who built a home on the lot right next to us. He soon discovered he was living next door to a house filled with people who had AIDS. He was not happy. He went to the city and tried to shut us down. It was a really bad scene.

I went out and talked to him. And this how that conversation went:

"Hi. How much did it cost you to build your house?"

He replied, "$180,000."

I said, "Move."

I wrote him a check for $180,000 and he moved. End of story.

I am not a patient guy. I didn't want to spend the next twenty years arguing with our next-door neighbor. Within time, I bought the corner house adjacent to that house plus the empty lot in between, with the idea of one day constructing a building on all that land. With three houses on one block and an empty lot, we were then Josue Homes.

We ended up opening seven houses total. But after I retired in 2011, they sold all the individual houses and brought the program into one of our downtown buildings.

Some people thought it was named Josue Homes for a

person named Josue. But that wasn't the case. Sister Fay originally named it "Josue House" because in the Bible, Josue means "God is salvation." In other words, He's with us. And that was the whole purpose of the program—for people with AIDS to know God was with them.

62.

Adjacent Monopoly

Before Josue Homes started and a bit before the St. Vincent de Paul Joan Kroc Center on 16th Street opened, we were kicked out of the Travelator because they wanted to sell the building. We needed to quickly find another housing solution to be able to continue helping our neighbors in need until we could move everyone into our new building. We ended up leasing an entire apartment building on 17th Street, one block east of our main site. We used that apartment building for housing until St. Vincent de Paul Joan Kroc Center opened. Once it was operational, we moved out of the rented apartment building and into our newly constructed center.

It was by way of being kicked out of the Travelator and being forced to scramble to find another building to rent to keep everything going that I resolved to never, ever rent again. To do the work we were doing, we needed to own all our buildings. When you rent, you have no control. The building owner has control. But when you own the building, you have control. No one can kick you out of something you own.

We needed to have long-term solutions. Owning the land and our buildings was the way we'd ensure our programs could continue without anyone else telling us we had to move. I realized then more than before just how valuable it was that we owned the entire block where we built our first housing development, a block that would continue to be developed into more housing in the years to come. Since we were immediately at capacity when we opened St. Vincent de Paul Joan Kroc Center, plans to build more housing went into motion right away, which of course meant we needed to raise more money.

Within two years of opening St. Vincent de Paul Joan Kroc Center, we remodeled an adjacent warehouse we owned to create another housing solution that could accommodate 150 men. Named in honor of Bishop Maher, we called it St. Vincent de Paul Bishop Maher Center. This building was a great addition at the time, because not everyone was ready for the programs we were offering; some simply needed a place to stay overnight. Okay, that's fine. We built a new building to meet their needs.

But by repurposing that warehouse to be housing, we then needed another warehouse. So we bought one immediately across the street, a former warehouse for ice. That meant we owned one city block plus half a block across the street and had two housing developments operating to meet the needs of our neighbors experiencing homelessness.

Next thing I knew, I was becoming a land developer. I went from being a parish priest to a charity fundraiser, housing provider, and land developer in a relatively short period of time despite not having any formal training for most of my new roles. When I was in seminary, they didn't teach all the business stuff we'd need to know when we got into our parish lives, yet we were responsible for a lot of business-oriented work—fundraising, management, development— in addition to everything else. The business of the parish is all stuff we had to learn on-the-job. Sometimes, priests don't want to handle the business side of parish life. But it's necessary. You can't turn on the lights in the church or parish hall without money coming in, so you have to be a fundraiser. Parish priests learn on-the-job and I was a learning with each new aspect of the job I had.

Being in charge of St. Vincent de Paul provided me with plenty of learning opportunities. Every day, I learned by making decisions. Sometimes my decisions were spot on and other times they weren't. When it worked out, great. I learned what worked and we did more of that. When it didn't, I learned what didn't work and we did something different moving forward. Not every decision I made ended up being the right decision, but I learned from each and kept going.

One valuable thing I learned about business when I was a parish priest that carried over to development work with St.

Vincent de Paul was how important it was to buy adjacent properties. If you want to grow, you have to have the space to grow, and for us that meant buying more properties next to what we already owned. The Pastor at Our Lady of Grace Parish did that. Whenever a house came up for sale that was next to the parish, he bought it. That's how they have a large property now. St. Rita's Parish did the same thing. When they needed a bigger hall, they built a second one on an adjacent property they had purchased. When they needed an even bigger hall, they built another one. They grew to having three halls plus their church all together. Then, one day the grocery store across the street went out of business and they bought that property and built yet another hall.

The key to our development at St. Vincent de Paul was buying and building on adjacent properties. So when Monsignor Topping purchased the parking lot city block of land in downtown San Diego in the early 1980s, there was plenty of land adjacent to it where we could build, which is what we've been doing since the first building opened in 1987.

Years down the line, when a new Bishop was assigned, and after we had acquired more and more properties, it was decided we'd transition St. Vincent de Paul Center into a newly established non-profit organization renamed St. Vincent de Paul Villages.

63.

One Dollar Building

In the early 1990s, the apartment building we had rented on 17th Street after being kicked out of the Travelator became a topic again because it was for sale. At the time, all US federal savings and loans banks were in crisis. They were being closed and all assets liquidated. The Resolution Trust Corporation (RTC) was a federal government-owned asset management company that was in charge of closing down all the banks and selling off their assets, which included selling off properties and closing out mortgage loans. One of the properties they were trying to get rid of was the 17th Street apartment building. The RTC contacted us since we were the most recent prior tenant and we had a big presence downtown as a builder by then.

The apartment building was proving to be hard for RTC to sell because it had a reputation as being a prostitution and drug center. It hadn't been well taken care of and it was rundown. No one wanted it, and I knew that. When the RTC contacted me, they offered the building at a purchase price of $1 million. To me, it wasn't worth that at all. I said, "No. I'll take it for $350,000."

Typical negotiators, we went back and forth for a bit, and they finally responded, "We'll take $675,000 for it."

By then, I was over it. The price was too much and I didn't want to deal with RTC anymore. They were trying to get way too much money out of a building no one wanted that needed a ton of work. I just wanted them to go away. I told my staff, "Tell them I will buy the building for one dollar. That's my final offer."

I figured we'd be done with it after that, and they'd go away. But not so fast. They came back and said they'd take one dollar for the building. Excuse me, what? I wasn't serious, but okay, one dollar it is. Sold! That's how we ended up buying an entire apartment building for a dollar.

Yet, since that one-dollar building needed a lot of work, we had to do a complete overhaul. One of our board chairs at the time was a retired Marine; he got a few guys from the Marine Corps Recruit Depot to gut the entire building, down to the basic interior structure. Then, we rebuilt it to be suitable housing.

But we couldn't do any of that until we got all the tenants out—tenants who were running illegal drug and prostitution businesses out of their apartments. We couldn't evict them just because we owned the building. That's not how it works. Tenants have rights and they all knew it. For any building owner, if you want tenants to move out, you have to subsidize them for their new place, which basically means you have to pay them to leave. We didn't want to do that.

The other option is to do what we ended up doing, which was make them want to leave on their own. We made it very difficult for them to keep living as they had been living. We placed security officers at the gate entrance to the building twenty-four hours a day. Whenever someone came to the building to visit a tenant, the guest was required to show their ID and we'd make a copy of it. Now, if you were going into the building to buy drugs or a prostitute, both of which were illegal, you probably didn't want some security officer knowing your identity. Eventually, all the customers stopped coming.

Also, since we didn't have a place to keep our German Shepherds at night, we had the dogs that were part of the security team for our other housing centers one block over go there every night; there was an outdoor space on the property well suited for them. So imagine, you wouldn't want to be sneaking out of the building with German Shepherd security guard-trained dogs onsite. We just made it miserable for the tenants to be there doing what they were doing, and eventually everyone moved out.

Ever since we reopened that building after remodeling, it has been used for transitional housing, hosting fifty apartments. Then following the adjacent property concept, we eventually bought the house next door to that apartment building on the west side, which was used as a guest house for a few years for visitors. We also bought the two empty lots adjacent to that guest house that would later become our parking lot and a gated playground for our children's center. Then we bought the adjacent property to the east of the apartment building, the corner lot, that would later become Villa Harvey Mandel Apartments, offering long-term housing solutions. We also bought up land across the street to the east, which is used for our maintenance center and another parking lot.

Plus, within a few years, an old historic home in the middle of the block on the 16th Street side came up for sale and we bought that, too. I have called that house my home for about twenty years. It has been really convenient to live directly across the street from St. Vincent de Paul Villages and all the adjacent properties we built over the years. Now here's the thing about my house. First, it sits on a fault line that runs right through my living room. Second, since it is designated as a historic home, we can't alter it at all. But the building rights that go with the land the house sits on can be transferred to an adjacent property if we desire. That means the fifty-unit apartment building we purchased for only one dollar that is currently three stories high can one day be rebuilt to be a high-rise—up to fourteen stories of housing.

Years down the line, we tore down the "ice house" warehouse and built more housing on that property. It's where the St. Vincent de Paul Villages Paul Mirabile Center was constructed with 350 beds for short-term housing, a medical center, job training center, and computer center. The Mirabile family's generous gift came at an important time, and I credit former board chairman David Malcolm and his wife Annie for helping to make that happen. Now, we needed another warehouse facility yet again. So we bought a distribution warehouse a few miles away on E Street, and that is where our offices were for a long time.

Eventually, the Bishop Maher Center was rebuilt to be our 15th and Commercial building. The mixed-use housing development offers a state-of-the-art approach to three-buildings-in-one: a child development center, transitional housing, and sixty-four apartments for supportive housing.

I am greatly simplifying a lot of work that was done over the course of a few decades of buying, funding, and building housing projects just to make a point about adjacent properties. When you look at an aerial view of east downtown, you'll see we have built housing on a really significant portion of it—on land we own. Just like in the game of Monopoly where you need to buy up as many adjacent properties as possible to then be able to build on them, that is what we did in our corner of downtown San Diego. We bought up adjacent properties and built housing on the land with the purpose of meeting the needs of our neighbors experiencing homelessness. At the moment, we are one of the top twenty land developers in downtown San Diego—all of which started from a warehouse thrift store and an empty city block parking lot.

64.

Vegas MASH Village

Over the years, many groups came to study our work with the desire to replicate our programs and our approach in their own cities. It makes me feel happy to know what started in downtown San Diego to help neighbors in need has expanded into other areas. Some of those housing solutions and programs still exist today. But there's one we got involved with in the mid-1990s that was started with the best of intentions but no longer exists: Father Joe's MASH Village—Mobile Assistance and Shelter for the Homeless.

The city of Las Vegas contacted us with a plan to build a new homeless shelter on large plot of land it owned. They wanted to hire us to run it for them. The pitch was that they'd build it and when it was all ready to go, we'd come in and manage it. The original deal we set up with them was that we'd get paid $500,000 per year for five years in exchange for managing all aspects of the shelter, including duplicating our programs there. Then, at the end of that period, we'd own the building outright and we'd continue to run it, helping Las Vegas residents experiencing homelessness and poverty. But that is not what ended up happening. There were some key things that contributed to what ended up being the failure of MASH Village and ultimately resulted in the building's destruction.

For one thing, we were not involved in the building design or construction at all. The group that was hired to design the building had not consulted with us. Since it was a city-funded and directed building project, we weren't involved in any of the construction process at all, either. Yet, it didn't seem strange to me since it was Las Vegas, which is a builder's paradise. There are construction projects going on in that city constantly, most of which are quality-built high-rises specifically constructed and designed for providing fantastic accommodations.

When the day came for me to go out there and tour the newly constructed housing building, one major thing was missing. It didn't have a kitchen! As I walked around the dining area with Vince Bartolotta, our chairman at the time, we kept opening doors looking for the kitchen, but we couldn't find it. After opening what turned out to be another storage closet, I asked, "Where's the kitchen?"

The person who was touring us around said they didn't build a kitchen for the shelter. You should have seen the look on my face. Shocked, I said, "What? There has to be a kitchen. How are you intending to serve hundreds of meals every day without a kitchen?"

The decision that was made by those in charge of the project's design and construction was that all meals would be brought in by a catering company. That did not make any sense to me whatsoever. On the bare minimum of meals, that meant they'd be bringing in hundreds of meals three times a day for the residents of the 180-bed shelter—not to mention those seeking daily services who were unsheltered. This decision was an expensive one that I'd never make. Also, since there was no kitchen onsite, there was no way to receive donated food from casinos and hotels, because the health code requires a kitchen on the premise to handle prep food for all consumable donations.

What would be discovered years down the line was that the building wasn't constructed to code. They cut a lot of corners during construction and didn't follow building codes. How were they able to do this? Well, the same people who were responsible for enforcing building codes owned the land and building, and were able to pass all their own inspections. Naturally, no one knew this until the building started falling apart and the corners of rooms were sinking.

Faulty construction aside, once new officials were elected, the deal made for us to own the building was rescinded. That infuriated me, especially since Father Joe's Villages in San Diego had been subsidizing MASH Village in Las Vegas to the tune of $1 million annually for a few years by that time. We had been losing money on the deal, but the prospect of owning the building kept me in it. When they took all that away, we gave our six-month notice that we'd be pulling out. And sure enough, a few months after we left, MASH Village was closed and the building torn down. Just like that.

As it turned out, Lady Luck was on our side in Las Vegas because owning that poorly constructed building would have been a huge loss for us.

65.

Martha's Kitchen and Village

I recall one day in the beginning of our involvement in Las Vegas, I was out there with Mary Case and a few other people from the board. We had all been in a series of meetings with the Las Vegas board members. Then, when we took a break before the next round of meetings focused on Village programs, I left and went home to San Diego. Mary later told me that the folks in Las Vegas were upset about me leaving; they questioned why the guy who was in charge would leave in the middle of the day. They didn't want to talk about programs without me there. With no mobile phones at the time, they couldn't reach me while on the road, of course, and Mary had to convince them I wasn't involved with developing and running Village programs, she was. Just like I mentioned earlier, Mary and her team were in charge of programs. They developed and ran programs, and I raised money for them.

Everything we created over the years was developed to run without me around. I don't need to be present for neighbors experiencing homelessness to get what they need. The entire one-stop-shop Village concept that's in San Diego can be replicated anywhere. Yet, too often over the years I have heard people in other cities say they couldn't do in their community what we've done in San Diego because they don't have a Father Joe. And honestly, take it from me, Father Joe, that's not correct at all.

It can be done and it has been done. That's exactly what happened in Indio, California with Martha's Village and Kitchen. Back in 1990, two women, Gloria Gomez and Claudia Castorena, started serving meals from their Catholic church's parish hall in Indio during the week. They couldn't serve on Saturdays and Sundays because the church is used on the weekends. Their desire was to have a facility where they could prepare and share food with people in the Coachella Valley who were in need seven days a week. They had a charity board that was interested in helping them do this and they came down to study what we did in San Diego. The board liked what we were doing and said they'd put the money up for funding the kitchen only if it was part of Father Joe's Villages.

Gloria and Claudia agreed to that. So, what started out with two women's hearts of service and compassion, just like Mary and Martha in biblical stories—with Mary often portrayed being close to Jesus as he taught and Martha being in the "kitchen" cooking meals for everyone—Martha's Kitchen and Village became part of Father Joe's Villages.

Modeled after what was created in downtown San Diego, we effectively duplicated all of our services and programs in Indio: housing, meals, medical, youth services, and more. For many years, San Diego's Villages helped subsidize Indio's Village. Then, after I retired, funding was shifted and the folks in Indio established their own organization as it exists today. Martha's Village and Kitchen is a fully operational, independent, self-sustaining agency that helps countless neighbors in need in their desert community. See, it works!

I recently spoke with Henry Burdick, who's the chairman of the board of Martha's Village and Kitchen right now, and he told me they are talking about expanding into other communities. Indio's experienced the positive impact of the one-stop-shop concept, which they refer to as continuum of care model, has on helping neighbors in need of rehabilitating and improving their lives. Indio's team desired to duplicate the people-first Village approach because they know it works. While they are just in early talks about possible expansion, knowing there are even discussions happening makes me happy and hopeful.

66.

Mammoth Sam

So much new construction and development was happening in downtown San Diego. Our original warehouse thrift store on the corner of 16th and Market streets even became a housing development. Back when we were still providing sandwiches daily from the thrift store's side door, the line was often so long that it extended down Market Street past Salazar's restaurant. It stands to reason that when people who are living on the street are waiting in line for food, and nature calls, odds are they aren't going to get out of line and go find a bathroom. They'd lose their place in line. It's common for someone to simply urinate where they are standing, which meant it was common for people standing in line by Salazar's to urinate on the sidewalk and in the bushes on his property.

So imagine, you are sitting at a table inside Salazar's eating your breakfast and looking out the window while chewing to see a homeless guy urinating in the bushes. Salazar's was not happy about this. Of course, I didn't want our neighbor unhappy with us, so I made some changes.

The solution we came up with was to shift the line to extend the other direction down 16th Street. Since we had already purchased the adjacent building next to the warehouse thrift store on that street, which was previously an industrial laundry facility, getting everyone to line up on the other street meant they'd be in front of our properties.

When the time was right, we tore down both buildings and built a brand new twelve-story housing complex with 136 units for families with fixed or low incomes. Many people who have graduated from our programs are able to live there. We call that building "SAM" since it's on the corner of 16th and Market.

But here's a little San Diego history you may not know. Before we were starting construction for the new building, the old buildings were torn down and the builders had to dig up the ground to be able to pour a deep foundation. During their digging, they discovered what turned out to be a tusk of a Columbian mammoth estimated to be 200,000 to 500,000 years old. That was the first mammoth fossil discovered in the area and the most complete and intact tusk ever found in the region.

Well, this mammoth created a big issue for us, because all construction had to stop until experts and archeologists came to the site to figure out what we were going to do with the mammoth tusk. If we wanted to keep it—since it was discovered on our property it was ours—we'd have to pay for all the fees associated with proper excavation and preservation, plus pay for all the experts and agencies involved. Or we could donate it to a museum and it would handle everything. Since we weren't in the business of fossil preservation, the decision was simple to have the San Diego Natural History Museum take over.

If you are ever walking around downtown San Diego and are at the corner of 16th and Market streets, go to the entrance of the building and you'll see a plaque on display that shares this story. As far as I know, the San Diego Natural History Museum still has the mammoth tusk in its possession and on display. While it was never officially named, we affectionately call our prehistoric neighbor Mammoth Sam.

67.

Cars, Boats, and Planes

Within about a twelve-year period of time, we bought and/ or built twelve different properties in San Diego County. One of the main ways we funded those purchases was through a concept we developed into being a $15 million a year fundraising program. A man who owned a parking lot and had been in the used car business came to us with a proposal to partner with him in selling donated vehicles. The concept was that we'd get cars donated to us, providing the donor with a tax deduction for the price of their car, and then this guy would sell the cars for us. We'd keep 90 percent of the money from the vehicle sale price and he'd keep 10 percent for his cut.

It seemed like a great idea to me, especially since we were already in that kind of business with our thrift stores. The concept was basically the same—seeking, receiving, and selling donated items—but this business model was with used cars instead of used clothing and furniture.

Right away, the car sales program was successful. Next thing you know, we were in the used car business. We're just like every other charity that needs to be raising money regularly to keep its main mission going. Selling used vehicles became a major funding source for us to continue developing housing projects and programs for our neighbors in need.

After the first year in business, I looked at the numbers and realized we were doing so much business that the guy who was selling the cars for us was making a lot of money from the deal. I decided I'd rather we do it ourselves. So, instead of continuing to outsource the job, we brought the program in-house and it became one of our main funding sources for the next decade. As more cars were donated to us, we had more cars to sell. The more cars we had to sell meant the more money we had to fund our work to help neighbors in need. This made sense to me. The solution was simple. We needed to get our hands on more inventory.

To get more cars, we needed to expand beyond San Diego. That meant we needed to get the word out to people in other cities. So, I did what I knew worked. I went back on television. I shot another commercial and it was advertised all throughout the US. I was on television day and night all over the country for years. By this time, I decided to ask for boats and planes as well. San Diego is a coastal city and we have a lot of boats in our waters so that made sense. I threw in asking for airplanes because it was different. Just like saying, "I am a hustler" on television made people stop and pay attention, saying I wanted your cars, boats, and planes made people stop and pay attention, too.

I recall one time I was preaching at a parish in Palm Springs and a couple from San Francisco came up after Mass to meet me. They told me they had been seeing me on television for years and just figured I was an actor playing a priest. They were surprised to find out I was a real priest. They asked, "Do people actually donate planes to you?" See, it worked.

Even many years down the line, when my long-time assistant Jose Gonzalez and I met former President Gerald Ford at charity golf tournament in Palm Springs, he referenced that commercial. Then, upon meeting the actor/comedian George Lopez at that same tournament, he did, too. It was incredible to me how far-reaching that commercial was. In fact, if there is a single reason people know about the work we are doing in San Diego to help our neighbors in need, all credit goes to that cars, boats, and planes commercial.

We were spending millions of dollars a year on advertising with an incredible return on that investment those first years. Our used vehicle sales program was hugely successful. Unfortunately, federal laws changed about how donated vehicles were valued and that negatively affected the program. Up until that point, if someone wanted to donate a vehicle to us from anywhere in the country, we'd go pick it up and give them a receipt noting its Blue Book value. At that time, everyone established a vehicle's value from Blue Book. It was standard.

For example, let's say you donated your car to us and its Blue Book value was $1,000. We'd give you a receipt for $1,000 in exchange for your donated car. Now, we might be able to sell that car for $1,200 or for only $500. To us, it was pure profit minus the expense of running the program. To you, it was a tax-deductible write-off for the value of your car regardless of what we were able to sell it for.

But the federal government decided that wasn't okay any longer and passed a law that no one in the country could give a donation receipt for a vehicle's value any longer; instead, it needed to reflect the actual sale price. This new law created a lot of issues for us because it would often take us a few months to sell a vehicle, which we usually did through our auctions.

Not only was this a lot more work for us to keep track of each vehicle to be able to send out receipts months later, but people didn't really like that they'd have to wait for their tax deduction only when and if we sold their vehicle for whatever price we could get for it. For many years, we'd get a lot of vehicles donated to us in November and December from people who wanted to reduce their taxable income. Prior to the law changing, we'd be able to give them a receipt immediately. With the changes, we wouldn't be able to get them the receipt for a while, which meant their tax filing would be delayed as they awaited proof of their deduction.

That law, combined with the passing of the clunker law, where all cars older than a certain year had to be destroyed and not sold, meant we were getting fewer vehicles donated. The program became less attractive to the donors and next thing we knew, it was only bringing in a fraction of what it once did.

But it had a great run. It was through all those donated cars, boats, and even two planes that we were able to keep buying up land. During that time, we even bought fourteen acres of land in Otay, California, which included a lot of space for us to park our vehicles before auction.

The program still exists. And while I am no longer popping up on your television as the hustler priest saying, "I want your cars, boats, and planes," people still recognize me because of that commercial. The power of television is incredible. Jose can tell you that it would happen almost every day for years that we'd be eating at a restaurant and within a few minutes, someone would walk up to us and say, "Aren't you that priest on TV?" Those commercials made me known, which made our work at the Villages known, and again, that was and always will be the whole point.

We even made the front page of the Wall Street Journal, but not for what you might think. A reporter was doing a story on drug smuggling at the Tijuana border. During his investigation, a car was detained that had drugs in it and when they got into the details of the car, they found it had been bought at one of our auctions. The officer mentioned that it was a Father Joe car. The reporter heard that and printed it. So there we were on the front page of the Wall

Street Journal getting press for our cars, and you know that old saying, "All press is good press." Well, there you go.

After I retired, I did another commercial to help raise money for the Villages with me looking into the camera saying, "I'm still here and I still want your cars, boats, and planes." There was great value in advertising. To think there was a time when we were spending a few million dollars on commercial advertising; it seems like a crazy amount of money to me now. But it was worth it, because what we were bringing in was exponentially more than that. Everyone who has donated vehicles to us has helped contribute to our success in creating housing solutions for neighbors in need.

68.

Compassionate Relief

While I was always seeking ways to earn money, I never put business above people. I have observed how that can be the case with other companies or organizations, where business is what matters most and people are secondary. That's not my way. And more importantly, that's not the way Jesus taught us to be. Jesus always put people first. That is what we are called to do if we are truly following his example. People are first. Our properties and programs exist because of people. People are our business.

When I was running things, if anyone came to our donation center warehouse and told my staff they didn't have any money and needed a bed or clothing, or whatever, I wanted my staff to do the compassionate thing and give them what they needed. Everyone on staff knew if someone came to us in need and we believed them, we'd give them what they needed. I never wanted us to turn anyone away or deny them. It didn't make any sense to me to deny someone in need only to turn around and sell an item that was donated to us for profit. If the person in need was standing in front of us, the compassionate thing to do was to help provide them with what they needed if we could. To always be compassionate was and always is the right decision in my book.

Also, my staff always knew they didn't need to call me to get permission to do the compassionate thing. Keith Mackay and Alex Miranda were my two long-time warehouse managers. Like everyone on the team, they were empowered to provide what was needed. But we weren't ignorant. There were times when people weren't being truthful and we knew it. We'd just redirect them to go through the normal channels.

Just the other day, I was talking with Alex, who visits me often because his wife Maria is my weekday caregiver, and he reminded me about how the warehouse staff would always put wheelchairs, crutches, and walkers off to the side, never to be sold. That way, whenever someone came to us in need for them, we had plenty to give. While Father Joe's Thrift Stores are a helpful part of creating revenue to help fund all of our programs, making a profit was never, ever prioritized over people.

In the early years, I found out after the fact about a time when we were at capacity at the Villages with no available beds. But a family came to the door in the middle of the night. It was raining outside and they needed a place to stay. Well, we happened to have a few cots in a storage closet and my staff let them in to sleep on them. The family was gone by the time I arrived in the morning. Do you think I was upset when I was told this story? No, I wasn't. I am glad they made a compassionate choice to provide relief to the family. While this isn't something that continued, it's an example of the standard of compassion my staff upheld as best as possible.

Something not many people know is that I'd hire undercover detectives to check up on my staff. Similar to how retail stores and restaurants hire people to act like customers— "secret shoppers"—to make sure staff members are providing excellent customer service, I did the same thing at St. Vincent de Paul Villages. At times, I would hire men and women undercover detectives to come in as if they were neighbors in need. They'd stay in our housing for a week or two and go through our whole process. They'd report back to me about what they experienced and how my staff conducted themselves. I wanted to make sure everyone on staff was providing our neighbors with compassion and respect. Seldom having any major issues to resolve, more regularly I'd hear stories of my staff going above and beyond to be helpful to meet their needs.

In everything we did, our job was to provide neighbors in need with compassionate relief. I truly believe a person can achieve what they want in life when they have the opportunity to do so. But if someone is stressing about whether or not they are going to have a bed to sleep on that night, they don't have energy to do much else. They are in pure survival mode. I felt our work was to help ease their burden. Once someone is out of survival mode, having a place to stay and food to eat, the work of rehabilitation can start and we were there to understand and meet their needs to help them improve their lives. And that's what happened over and over again!

We have so many success stories. One in particular I can think of is a woman who came to us with her children after escaping a domestic abuse situation. She had no job, no money, and nowhere to go. What did she need? She needed compassionate relief. She needed a place for them to stay, food to eat, care for her kids, counseling to get stronger emotionally, a recovery program to get sober, medical care, and job training. We had all that for her under one roof. She got sober. She got a job. Her children are educated with her oldest in college earning honors. God doesn't make junk! Our neighbors just need the opportunity to grow into their fullness and experience unconditional compassionate relief.

69.

The Best Thief I've Ever Known

There was one person who had my whole staff wrapped around her finger and that was Mother Antonia Brenner. She ran a prison ministry in Tijuana and was a compassionate servant to so many neighbors in need across the border. She'd arrive at our warehouse with an empty truck, seeking at first just few items, yet would drive away with a truck full of stuff. Keith would later tell me he just couldn't say no to her. And if you think I am a hustler, Mother Antonia was the best of the best. She could get anyone to open up their account and give. She lived compassion and joy every day.

Mother Antonia had been a socialite living in Hollywood. She had a whole other life raising a family before she became a nun. It was because of her other life that she wasn't allowed to be in any nun orders. But Bishop Maher was a progressive and compassionate man, and he let her form an order of one. She took a vow to Bishop Maher and started her own order. To provide compassion to prisoners in Tijuana, she grew her order— Eudist of the Eleventh Hour—to have over fifty nuns. Until the end of her life, she lived inside the La Mesa Prison in Tijuana, calling all the murderers and other criminals her sons and daughters, providing them with love and compassion every day. She was truly a remarkable woman.

I will never forget the day I met Mother Antonia, which was before she had any of us wrapped around her finger. She and her nuns had come into our thrift store on Market Street and my staff was a little annoyed because the nuns were acting like they deserved to get stuff from our store for free—almost like they were entitled to it. So, some of the nuns came upstairs to my office to talk to me, trying to persuade me into giving them everything they wanted. That annoyed me. The nuns told me Mother Antonia was downstairs and I could talk to her instead. I marched downstairs thinking I was going to give her a piece of my mind and put a stop to this.

I was wrong. As I walked up to Mother Antonia, she dropped to her knees and extended her hands up to me, saying, "Padre, your blessing please." And in that moment, I melted. I couldn't say no to her, and I never did. We became friends and together did our best to help neighbors in need. In the book written about her life, the section that mentions me is called, "The Best Thief I've Ever Known." She was remarkable at getting money from people, but it was your heart she stole with her love and compassion.

70.

Millions of Meals

Providing compassionate care with the most basic human needs of food and shelter is where everything started and has been constant for decades. Ever since opening our very first building that we built for neighbors in need in 1987, we have been providing more prepared meals to San Diegans than anyone else in the county consistently. In 1996, after being open for nine years, we celebrated successfully serving 10 million meals. I am unsure of what the number is now, over two decades later from that celebration, but I'd venture to say we've doubled or tripled that. I'd gamble that we are one of the top daily food service providers in San Diego, even with so many casinos, hotels, and restaurants in our county.

Also, I think it's important to point out here that whenever there has been an economic recession or health crisis, like what everyone experienced with the COVID-19 pandemic, it is common for many households to stop eating out at restaurants and minimize travel—which negatively impacts the food service industry. But guess what? Our daily meal service never goes down during times like that. Actually, it goes up. We consistently provide meals to neighbors in need experiencing homelessness and poverty. For decades, no matter what is happening in the world around us, we have been serving our neighbors with their most basic needs for survival: food and shelter.

Over the years, I have advocated for the importance of what we do for our neighbors in need, speaking out on radio and television talk shows and challenging politicians. So many people just don't get the expansive work we do and how it benefits everyone in our city, not just our neighbors in need, but entire industries. We create jobs! We have provided consistent jobs to San Diegans in almost every industry for decades and have been a consistent provider of solutions for what's needed for our community. We are an asset to San Diego.

I've experienced it a few times where someone running for a political office will campaign on the heartstrings of helping the homeless, but once elected, their agenda changes and their actions end up redirecting money that was previously funding programs for our neighbors in need. I have always been very vocal about the work we do, because our neighbors experiencing homelessness and poverty need advocates to be vocal and visible when decisions are being made.

A hard truth is that everyone loves what we do, but no one wants us in their neighborhood. When we started building in the east village of downtown San Diego back in the mid 1980s, no one bothered us. No one was building in that part of downtown except us. Over the years, all sorts of new high-rise buildings have been constructed near properties we've been in for decades. But, we've had some new neighbors get upset that we are here. Wait a minute. You just moved in. We've been here. You knew we were here. We're not going anywhere because we own our buildings and our land. Beyond that, you just bought a property worth $700,000 and we have about $100 million in building projects going on at any given time—creating a lot of jobs and housing for many San Diegans while purchasing materials and supplies from local companies. We are an asset! Not to mention, the city gets money for every person registered for the census. So our neighbors in need who are part of our residential programs are contributing to the city's economy. Again, we're an asset.

Beyond supporting our neighbors in need, we have helped during natural disasters. For example, when the Southern California wildfires happened a number of years ago, thousands of San Diegans were displaced and sent to the stadium as a hub. The agency that was leading some of the relief efforts was calling around to a bunch of us to see if we could help provide meals. They needed 6,000 meals served each day and hoped to get a few of us with industrial kitchens to provide up to 500 meals each. I called over to the guys who were running our kitchen, who just happen to be ex-Navy cooks, and they said, "Father Joe, we can do all 6,000 meals. It's just like a ship coming into port. Easy. We've got it." And they went to work cooking meals and helping our neighbors in need.

Back in the 1990s when the big earthquake hit Northridge, we were the first trucks up there. My guys told me it was eerie driving up through Los Angeles because no one was on the road; they were able to just drive right on through. That's never the case driving from San Diego to Los Angeles. But when the earthquake hit, we packed up the trucks with a bunch of supplies we always kept readily available in the warehouse—boxes of blankets, pallets of water, healthcare products—and off they went. There was no red tape to cut through. No one needed to "approve" them going. We just acted when there was a need.

I remember one time during another fire out in east San Diego, we set up a temporary meal service area as did a few other well-known national agencies. But all of the firefighters wanted to eat at Father Joe's because we were known for serving them good meals. From us they got steak and chicken and the works. From other agencies they got relief food like soup and sandwiches. With no unnecessary red tape in the way and the infrastructure to take immediate action, my team organized and prepared quality meals for everyone fighting those fires.

71.

Power of Presence and Creating Opportunities

In my life, something I have come to know through experience is how much presence matters. Making myself known through the media, being present on your television screen for years asking you to donate your vehicles to us, created opportunities for our work to be known. This allowed us to have more opportunities to help all of our neighbors in need. The public has to know what you are doing to have the opportunity to help.

While I am known to be a "hustler" for donations, I've only ever asked three people directly for money. Yes, only three! Yet by having a regular media presence, by being present at every fundraising event, and by sending out updates regularly through the mail, I was constantly present in your life—asking for your donations and your help without ever asking you directly for money. When I'd enter a room, just by my presence of being there, many people felt a stirring in their own hearts to help and donate or hide their wallets—

one of the two. But silliness aside, I have always made plenty of requests to an entire room or to the general public, but never asked directly. God took care of that.

Something I enjoy doing is talking with people and getting to know them. I am a great listener. I ask genuine questions and listen to what people have to say. And as you might assume, I've discovered a lot of creative opportunities in everyday conversations by paying attention to what's going on around me.

One time I was the Chaplain on a cruise ship, which put me in the position of having fascinating conversations during meals with a lot of interesting people. During one particular conversation, a woman was talking about how her late husband had been a painter. Naturally, I asked her what sort of painting he had done—thinking of painting canvases or something along those lines. She responded, "Oh, he painted aluminum cans. He invented the paint that is used on all soda and beer cans." I was fascinated! Have you ever wondered about that? I have been drinking cans of Pepsi every day for decades and had never thought about how they get their name and logo on them. We can learn a lot by simply asking questions and listening to what people have to say. Of course, she asked more about what I did and I told her. She was fascinated. She and I became friends and she ultimately ended up making a sizable donation to us— without me ever asking her directly to do so. The stirring to help was within her.

It's incredible to think about how many inventions like that exist—normal things we use and see every day that someone somewhere came up with the idea for. In fact, over the years we have received donations from the families of people who invented the hula hoop, the bobby pin, and more.

I have always been seeking ways for us to make money in creative ways. There is always a way to make a buck. Ever since I was a kid, I could see opportunities in everyday circumstances. When PSA Airlines went out of business in the late 1980s, I called and asked them if we could have all of their branded products: paper cups, paper napkins, and even the paper envelopes passenger tickets used to be put into at their airport. PSA wasn't going to need any of that anymore and had to get rid of it. They agreed to donate it to us. Then, I called a paper recycling company that paid a certain amount of money per pound for recycled paper and we struck a deal. They went and picked up all of the paper inventory from PSA, weighed it, and cut us a check for it. I never even touched PSA paper, except for the check when it was mailed to us.

In the 1990s, when Doug Manchester transitioned the marina hotel from being an InterContinental Hotel to a Marriott Hotel, all of the branded products needed to be changed. That meant all the InterContinental soaps, shampoos, and conditioners needed somewhere to go. At St. Vincent de Paul, we constantly had a need for personal hygiene items in handout sizes to be given to our neighbors in need, so he donated everything to us. Along with the name change, they decided to completely redesign most of the hotel, including the bar area. That meant all the tables and chairs needed to go. I liked those chairs a lot and asked Doug if I could have all of them for our chapel at St. Vincent de Paul Village. He agreed. To this day, those chairs are our chapel chairs. Since the bar had been named "Molly's" after his oldest daughter, we have always referred the chapel chairs as Molly's chairs.

72.

Christmas Joy

I just sent out my Christmas cards for the year. Some people may think sending out Christmas cards isn't that important anymore, but I do. I love sending and receiving them. I keep all the cards and photos I receive on display in my office for a few months. It brings me great joy to see everyone's well wishes and smiling faces every day.

When I was growing up, Christmas was always a joyful time. I have fond memories of Christmastime, even those years when my parents didn't have any money to buy us presents. Our family was all together; that's what mattered most to my mom, so that's what mattered to me. Some years, knowing there wasn't money for presents, I either worked to earn money or gambled to win money I could give to my brothers and sisters—money to buy presents for themselves. I loved playing the numbers and I knew the odds would be in my favor whenever I could outlast the other guy by having more money to start with. I'd take the money I earned from working and use it to gamble in street games. Sometimes I lost, but more times than not I won. I'd be able to give my siblings thirty or forty bucks each, which was a lot of money to us at the time, and they'd go to Alexander's clothing shop and pick out what they wanted. Then, they'd wrap it up and put it under the tree so everyone had something to open on Christmas morning.

Some years, my mom got our presents from the St. Vincent de Paul Society at our parish. There was a little store of donated stuff that parishioners or anyone in need could take. It was also through our parish's St. Vincent de Paul Society that my mom would get voucher cards to get food at local stores when we ran out of money. Instead of there being a pantry at the parish, these cards could be turned in at any food store and she could choose what she wanted— what we needed.

As a child, I was in the position to receive help from St. Vincent de Paul. As an adult, I was placed in the position to help people through St. Vincent de Paul. I am a great believer that history repeats itself and most things come full circle. I recall when I first got the job, I told all my siblings they had to start donating because we were once the family that needed help. It was our turn to provide for others. No one was excluded from my hustle for donations, including my family.

All this is to say that Christmas at St. Vincent de Paul Villages was always a big deal. I wanted everyone to have a joyful experience. Even the lobby of our first building was constructed with vaulted ceilings purposefully to be able to have a tall Christmas tree on display every year. The idea was always to put our tree in the highest part of the room, so when anyone walked in the front door, straight ahead would be a beautifully decorated Christmas tree welcoming them.

Imagine a young child who had been living in a car with their parent walking into St. Vincent de Paul Villages and not only having a bed to sleep in, warm showers to clean themselves, hot meals to eat, and a courtyard playground, but also a towering Christmas tree lit up with the magic of the season. Suddenly it isn't the worst time of the year for them. "Do we really get to stay here?" That feeling of Christmas joy is what we focused on providing.

For many years, the Ladies Guild organized two really special Christmas events for Village families. Santa's Workshop was an event where parents would be able to shop for presents to give to their children. We received thousands of donated new toys and clothing each year, and the ladies would organize them all by value on shelves in one of our warehouses. Then, parents would be brought in to shop for items for their children. The ladies would help them wrap the presents and we'd deliver a bag of presents to each room on Christmas Eve so when the children woke up Christmas morning, they had a bag full of presents to open from their parents.

It was always important to me that the presents came from the parents, not us. Again, this was all about helping people feel good about themselves when they were with us. A child's perspective of their mom and dad is of them being heroes. The parents feel good that they have provided for their children.

The Ladies Guild organized a Christmas Festival each year for the children with game booths and pictures with Santa. There was a store of items for children to pick out presents to give to their parents. The children would help wrap the presents so Mom and Dad had packages to open Christmas morning too. Everyone got to experience the magic and joy of Christmas.

While these two events have been changed in the years since I retired, the spirit of giving and helping others remains during Christmas and throughout the year. Focusing on the needs of children is just as important as focusing on the needs of adults. That's why every building we have constructed has a playground built into it.

Recalling my days of running around on the roof of St. Joseph's church in the Bronx, I made sure children staying in St. Vincent de Paul Villages had a place to play and that's why some of our buildings have enclosed playgrounds on rooftops or built into the children's floors. The 15th and Imperial building has three floors dedicated to youth and each one has an age-appropriate playground—built especially for a specific age group to enjoy as they learn and are cared for.

From infants to seniors, and every age in between, I believe we have done great work for our neighbors, meeting them where they are and providing opportunities to improve their lives. While not everyone wants to be helped or wants to go the distance to graduating from our programs, I believe we have done and continue to do what Jesus desires for us all to do and provide for our neighbors in need.

73.

Toussaint Teens

Some of those neighbors who needed our help were teenagers. Some of the teens were runaways or had been kicked out of their homes and were living on the streets. Others had been kids who came up through our Village programs and needed a next step of care their parents couldn't readily provide yet. Teens were falling into a gap where housing and programs were scarce because government funding wasn't available for their age group. Once we realized this, we went to work to figure out a solution.

Most government funding at that time directed to helping homelessness was focused on programs for adults. So it's easy to see that with the greater portion of government money being directed to adult-focused programs, the bulk of agencies focused on offering programs and services to help adults experiencing homelessness. That's why our work with youth has always been so important. No one else was attempting to provide services to all age groups under one agency umbrella approach like we were, mainly because there wasn't funding for it all. But if the only thing standing in our way from helping teens was money, I knew we could solve that by raising it ourselves. And that's what we did.

We named Toussaint Academy after one of my heroes, Pierre Toussaint, who was a Haitian-American hairdresser, philanthropist, and former slave who lived in the late 1700s and early 1800s. When he was freed from slavery, he took the last name of "Toussaint" in honor of the hero of the Haitian Revolution who established that nation. Pierre Toussaint became very wealthy. He and his wife took in orphans and provided shelter for many homeless teens while helping them get an education and learn a trade. He was the first layperson to be buried in the crypt below the main altar of St. Patrick's Cathedral on Fifth Avenue in New York City. Naming our teen housing and education center after him was important to me.

To get Toussaint started, we first used a building that was owned by our board chairman at the time, Larry Cushman. Then, a little while later, we bought a building especially for our teens. I recall driving through downtown one day and noticing a building I thought would be perfect for teenagers, mainly because it had an outdoor stoop area where they could hang out. I called our real estate broker and told him I wanted to buy the building. He was confused at first because it wasn't located close to our other downtown buildings, and it wasn't actually for sale. I told him that didn't matter, and asked him to find out who owned it and have them name their price.

As timing would have it, the day he made the call was also the day the two partners who owned the building were in an argument about what to do next with it. Then, out of the blue, they get a call from us saying we want to buy it. Just like that, the next thing you know, we owned the building. It needed quite a bit of work, so we orchestrated a big media push and fundraising campaign. Basketball legend Magic Johnson came into town to be part of it.

As far as housing goes, we could only legally house thirty teens in residence. We did that, and also rented out the other rooms as apartments. That way, graduates of our program could remain there and weren't shuffled back out onto the street. They could continue having a place to live as they found jobs and went to college, having the opportunity to become a success.

Toussaint Academy offered schooling for middle and high school-aged students, and teens could earn their diplomas. We empowered them to take pride in themselves and their home. We provided opportunities for them to do new things as incentives for earning good grades and doing their residential chores. Toussaint teens may have had to deal with some adult experiences in their lives, but most of them had not had the chance to have fun teenage experiences and that's what we offered them.

One of the enrichment incentives we offered included doing outdoor activities: camping, hiking, canoeing, and even snowboarding. Many of the teens had never done any of those things. Ryan Hudson, a teenager who was part of Toussaint Academy, went snowboarding for his first time through a program we offered. He took to it right away. Now, Ryan is a professional snowboarder and has been endorsed by some major companies. He sent me a hat a while ago he designed for his own clothing line. I couldn't be happier knowing Ryan is living a full life after being a kid who came up through our program; he empowered himself to be successful doing what he loves to do.

Another fun thing our teens got to experience was attending concerts. Teenagers love music and we had a number of special opportunities for them to go to concerts, which many of them never had been able to do before. I recall one year when Bruce Springsteen came to town. He's done a lot of work helping teens living on the streets. For his concert, he invited a few teen centers to be special guests including Toussaint. We were able to get into the concert early and had great seats. The teens were excited, but honestly it was my staff that couldn't hold it together. Everyone on staff wanted to meet "The Boss." After the show, he called up and said he wanted to drop by to see Toussaint, which he did. Again, my staff were beside themselves.

Toussaint was shut down after I retired. The funding just wasn't there any longer because it had been mainly funded through our cars, boats, and planes program. This is an important point to make about how much changes in government policies can negatively impact programs. We received some backlash about closing Toussaint, but like some of the other programs that were shut down after I retired, the large revenue stream we had from vehicle sales just wasn't there anymore. This is why I have always done my best to be active in politics, both on the regional and national levels. It's been essential to have visibility and a voice in all matters where governing bodies are creating policies and laws that impact our work helping neighbors in need.

Even though Toussaint has been closed for a number of years, I often receive updates about our teens who made successes of themselves. In fact, just the other day I received an email about one of our Toussaint residents who just became a doctor. Dr. Anthony Lopez and his wife, who is a medical doctor, live in Ventura, California. So, the seeds of empowerment planted in our Toussaint teens continue to help them grow and experience the fullness of life.

In 2013, a couple years into my retirement, I was honored with receiving the Congressional Medal of Honor Society's Citizen Service Above Self Award. It was by far the most humbling experience of my life. That year, they decided to honor six local heroes, and I was one of them. The gentleman who put the medal on me was a decorated war hero who was an amputee from combat. When he leaned down to put the medal around my neck he said to me, "You are my hero."

Wow. I was stunned. That's how I felt about him. He's the

one who did the hard stuff in combat. To me, I'm just a guy who did a job. But I guess that's what he'd say, too, that he was just doing his job. When we all do "our job" in this life, helping each other and giving to each other, we become everyday heroes for each other.

To know some of our Toussaint teens have become doctors, teachers, entrepreneurs, professional athletes, and more feels good. They, too, are everyday heroes who just needed someone to believe in them. That is what we tried to do for them at Toussaint Academy.

74.

People Are The Village

For me, this is what it's all about. Knowing our work has made a difference in people's lives in some positive way helps me know what we have done and continue to do matters. I have spoken with many US presidents, including President George Bush Sr., when he recognized me receiving a Thousand Points of Light Award. Over the years, I have received countless awards on the regional and national level. I have been named Best (fill-in-the-blank) of the Year by magazines and organizations. And while all of those special things are nice, they aren't what I care most about. What matters to me is knowing the work we have done and continue to do helps improve lives! Nothing compares to the feeling of having someone tell me their life was improved through the opportunities we've provided for them to grow into their own fullness.

There is no greater joy in the world to me than to have a server or a chef in a restaurant come up to me and say with pride, "Hi Father Joe. I am graduate of St. Vinnie's." We made a difference in people's lives and continue to do so, and that's what matters most.

After I retired, they renamed St. Vincent de Paul Villages to be Father Joe's Villages. Since every city has a St. Vincent de Paul of some sort, this name change helps differentiate the work being done at the Villages from others. But it's never been about me. I didn't do it alone. In many ways I was just the bobblehead—the guy who was willing to put himself out there in the media as a "hustler priest" and be made into a plastic bobblehead doll as a fundraising gimmick. I was just one of many people who helped transform lives with compassion, respect, empathy, empowerment, and dignity.

Father Joe's Villages exist because countless people made the choice to help neighbors in need and continue to do so. Everyone is the village! Everyone has come together to build the Villages, and my hope for the future is that everyone continues to support and help our neighbors in need.

Thousands upon thousands of volunteers of all ages have graced us with their presence, providing their love and time to help neighbors in need. Many youth organizations, scouting troops, and school groups have volunteered with us on their spring and summer breaks, and continue to do so year after year. As I mentioned earlier, the first group that organized to volunteer to serve meals at the Villages was Congregation Beth Israel. Our Jewish neighbors have been serving meals to our neighbors in need every Sunday since 1987. Why do people keep coming back to help? Because everyone is the village!

It has always been important to me to recognize everyone who's donated to us. When you tour Father Joe's Villages, you will see plaques on the walls with names of people who have provided financial donations. While some of our buildings are named for our major donors, I made sure for many years that any person who donated to us regularly got recognized with their names on plaques that hang on the walls of our buildings.

I recall when we opened our first building, there was an elderly woman there who had been donating half of her government-issued block of cheese to us each week. There she stood near Joan Kroc; both women had generously given what they had to give to help neighbors in need. Whether by way of money being donated or time being volunteered, there are so many wonderful people who have helped build and sustain Father Joe's Villages.

One of the original members of our Ladies Guild is Dottie Cunningham. She heard me speak at one of the first churches I preached at about the project back in the mid 1980s and from that day forward she has volunteered selflessly to help neighbors in need. Her career was in nursing and I will never forget the day I walked into our medical clinic to see Dottie on her knees washing the feet of a neighbor in need. That vision stays with me because moments like that happened every day. It was normal. Neighbors helping neighbors in need, just as Jesus taught us.

While there are plenty more stories I could share and there are countless names of wonderful people not mentioned within the pages of this book, I hope this collection of my life stories gives you a glimpse into who I am and perhaps provides some seeds of inspiration for your own life.

I am nearing my eightieth birthday. I have lived a good life. I have traveled. I have made many friends. I have been blessed beyond measure. I am happy! Even as I am confined to a wheelchair now, I am limited but I haven't stopped. I continue to attend Boy Scout award ceremonies and respectfully attend funerals of those who have passed. I enjoy having lunch with visitors and occasionally giving tours of Father Joe's Villages for donors. I love being able to have video calls with all my brothers and sisters, who I love very much.

I looked in the obituaries this morning and my name wasn't there. I'm alive. I am blessed. It's another great day. I will keep going until the day Jesus calls me home. I believe I've done my best to live my life as Jesus desired this poor kid named Joey Carroll from the Bronx to live. Whenever my day comes to leave this life, I will be ready. Until then, I am still here and I am ready to be a hustler for my neighbors in need.

As I mentioned in the beginning of this book, my gravestone has already been prepared. It simply says: He was a good priest.

I don't think I've been a great priest or an exceptional or

inspirational priest. I've been a good priest, and good is good enough.

Photos

The Carroll family in the Bronx

Playing curb ball

We played tag on the roof of
St. Joseph's church.

Who's that?

Mom and Dad

Being a tourist with Mom, cousin Anna, and sister Eileen
during my stay at USD.

With my loving mom, Kitty Carroll, the day I became a priest.

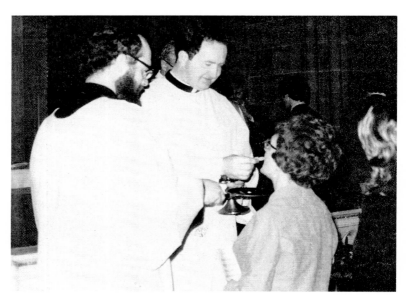

At my ordination, the first person I served
Communion to was my mom.

The Carroll brothers (left to right): Jack, Jim, Joe, and Tom

With my sisters (left to right): Eileen, Peggy, Kathleen, and Patsy

All four Carroll brothers were Best Campers at
"Camp Choate" (Saint Andrews Camp).

The Cotto family at the first Eagle Scout Awards
ceremony I conducted.

While growing up, everyone said I'd be a priest. They were right.

Honoring the accomplishments of our youth matters to me.
This is one of the Girl Scout and Boy Scout Awards ceremonies
we had at Our Lady of Grace (OLG) church.

Bishop Maher was supportive
of scouting and helped at
ceremonies.

With Kathryn Cloward (author) at
OLG for her First Communion.

No matter where we were camping or retreating,
we always had Sunday morning Mass.

I am a Boy Scout for life.

My best friend, Monsignor Terry Fleming

My friend, Archbishop Salvatore Cordileone

Spaghetti dinners at the Travelator

Donated items to be sold at our thrift store

St. Vincent de Paul Joan Kroc Center was designed to resemble the California Missions.

The real Padre talking with the San Diego Padres on the Roger Hedgecock Show, with a Pepsi within reach.

Built from scratch, my idea became reality.

Bishop Maher blessing the new St. Vincent de Paul Joan Kroc Center
with Joan, Amanda (her granddaughter), and a TV news
camera person next to me.

World Habitat Awards

Chairman Jim Mulvaney

Archbishop of Canterbury and
Monsignor Dennis Mikulanis

Archbishop of Canterbury and
Ladies Guild members Connie
White, Ginnie Rische,
and Mary Codling

Bishop Leo T. Maher

The St. Vincent de Paul Ladies Guild members
Pictured with Mary Sue Davis, Barbara Bixel, and Ruth Dumond

Sister Fay and Dottie Cunningham

Basketball legend Magic Johnson attended the first
Toussaint Academy event. Pictured with Mary Case (stripes)
and Chairman Vince Bartolotta (behind)

Bruce Springsteen provided Toussaint Academy with concert tickets
and spent time with everyone. Pictured with
Diane Plaster, Mary Case, and Harvey Mandel

Meeting the Pope in Rome

An event honoring Joan Kroc with Bishop Robert Brom
and Father Theodore Hesburgh

Cardinal Hayes High School 50-year reunion

"I'm here to hustle you out of money."

Walking in Lisdoonvarna, Ireland

Dining in Ireland with Sister Pat Walsh, Diane Plaster,
and Larry Plaster

A humbling moment as a hero said I was his hero.

Congressional Medal of Honor Society's
Citizen Service Above Self Award

Mary and Terry Case

Father Gilbert Gentile, Trinitarian Sisters of Mary,
and Sister Carmel Lohan (right with bag)

Kathryn Cloward and Mary Cloward, my first secretary

Mother Antonia Brenner, "The Best Thief I've Ever Known"

The hat designed by Toussaint Academy graduate and
professional snowboarder, Ryan Hudson

My family (left to right): Kathleen and Gyula, Eileen, Jim and Ann, Peggy and Nick, Patsy, Tom, and Ginger and Jack

Doctor Carroll

Father Joe

Special Thanks

For providing photos shared in this book,
special thanks to:

The Carroll Family
Mary Case
Mary Cloward
Dottie Cunningham
Father Chuck Fuld
Father Gilbert Gentile
Margot Meier Howard
Maria Miranda
Claudia Moran
Larry and Diane Plaster

For providing publishing and proofreading assistance,
special thanks to:

Mary Cloward
Jennifer Collins Peinert

For viewing photos in color and more, go to:
FatherJoeHustlerPriest.com

Father Joe
Life Stories of a Hustler Priest

Request for Amazon Reviews

Did you find aspects of this book interesting or insightful?
Was there something shared that inspired you or helped you?
Were you shocked or moved by any of the stories?
Did you ever laugh out loud reading about Father Joe's life?

It would be greatly appreciated if you'd write and share
an honest review of this book on Amazon.

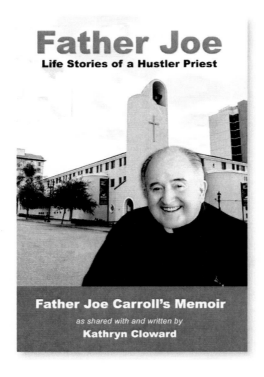

Author's Note

I met Father Joe when I was two months old, when he came to Our Lady of Grace as our parish priest. He was very present in my family's life, and my mom was his first secretary at St. Vincent de Paul. A lot of my clothes were bought at the St. Vincent de Paul Thrift Store, including my favorite purple tracksuit—an outfit I wore so much that my softball coach nicknamed me "Kathryn the Grape."

Decades later, I brought that nickname and outfit to life in an illustrated series. Through my Kathryn the Grape storytelling, I introduce children to social and emotional well-being tools for understanding and expressing their feelings, making mindful choices, and being kind and compassionate to themselves and others.

In March 2019, I attended a fundraising event at Father Joe's Villages with my mom. After Father Joe learned what I did for a living, he nodded his head, paused for a moment, and said, "Kathryn, I have a book I'd like for you to write."

We met for the first time to discuss the book on April 12, 2019—Father Joe's 78th birthday. This book released exactly two years later on April 12, 2021. I wrote it in first person in Father Joe's voice because I want you to feel as if you're sitting with him, listening to him tell his story. I got to experience firsthand what it's like to work with Father Joe, and it's been one of my life's greatest honors. I joyfully dedicated two years of my life to writing Father Joe's book in service of honoring him and his legacy.

If you've enjoyed reading Father Joe's life stories in this book and you'd like a child you love to know about Father Joe's goodness, Father Joe's Six Golden Seeds—a Kathryn the Grape youth version of his story as a book and song—is available at Amazon.com and KathrynTheGrape.com for everyone to enjoy.